Unquiet Spirits of Worcestershire

by

Anne Bradford

Hunt End Books

Hunt End Books

66 Enfield Road, Hunt End, Redditch
Worcestershire, B97 5NH, England
Telephone: 01527 542516
e-mail: anne.bradford@tesco.net

31 October 1999
ISBN 0-9519481-5-6

Photographs by John and Anne Bradford
Cover and book design by John Bradford

Made and printed in Great Britain by
Redwood Books Ltd
Kennet Way
Trowbridge, Wiltshire
BA14 8RN

Acknowledgements

Thanks should first go to all those who have contributed paranormal experiences, without which this book could not have been compiled.

Also:
Irene Orlik for help and advice;
Rose Fitzpatrick for nagging me to continue writing and publishing;
Bill Kings for the old Bromsgrove ghost stories;
Alan Lauder, of Kidderminster ghost walks (01562 630046), who has passed many ghost stories on to me;
Redditch Pictorial Society (especially Phillip Coventry and Alan Foxall) for old photographs;

librarians at Redditch (especially Philip Davis), Bromsgrove, Worcester and Kidderminster;

Tourist Information Centres at Redditch, Kidderminster, Malvern and Droitwich.

The following newspapers and radio stations have also been involved:

Berrows Worcestershire Journal, Bromsgrove Messenger, Droitwich Advertiser, Evesham Admag, Evesham Journal, Kidderminster Shuttle, Kidderminster Express and Star, Redditch Advertiser, Redditch Standard, Upton News, Worcester Evening News;

BBC West Midlands (Ed Doolan, Jenny Wilkes, Tony and Julie, and Carl Chinn)
BBC Hereford and Worcester (Mike George, Jill Manley, Rob Yarnold)

CONTENTS

WORCESTERSHIRE VILLAGES

Note: An asterisk after a name denotes the use of a pseudonym.

PREFACE

I developed a passion for ghost stories about the age of eleven when I read 'The Monkey's Paw' by W W Jacobs. While my friends were reading Angela Brazil or the *Just William* stories, I was scouring the library bookshelves looking for tales of mystery and imagination. In later years, the writings of M R James rekindled my enthusiasm. Then in 1992, I was looking through the library archives with our local history librarian, Philip Davis, when I happened to notice a collection of local Victorian ghost stories. They captured the history of the Redditch area in a way no historian could hope to emulate. They gave you the 'feel' of the times; the gossip, the preoccupations, the beliefs, the hopes, the fears, the day-to-day minor events. Philip mentioned that he was looking for someone to update and publish them, and I volunteered. I got hooked again. This is now my sixth book on the subject and I have lost count of the number of lectures on 'Ghosts, Murders and Scandals' that I have given to various groups ranging from Young Wives to Senior Citizen's societies.

One aspect of ghost stories which I particularly enjoy is their involvement with history. As soon as anyone experiences 'something peculiar' he/she starts delving into the history of the vicinity to try to find some kind of cause or explanation. Ghost stories add flesh to the basic historic facts to make history more interesting. Put a ghost story with a piece of history and even a teenager sits up and takes notice. I like to think that, as I'm putting these ghost stories down on records, I'm capturing something of the history of our time. They cover all life's rich tapestry - birth, adolescence, work, leisure, relationships, sex, religion, death.

I am often asked how I manage to collect all these anecdotes. Sometimes listeners to one of the local radio stations are kind enough to telephone me with a story after I have been on air. However, most of the stories come from my lectures. With any luck, we will all sit down for a chat at the end of a lecture and I hear the local gossip. I take the telephone number of anyone with a story and telephone them during the week. I follow up and research as many facts as possible but if every one were to be investigated the book would never be written!

I am also often asked if I have any rational or scientific explanations for these strange phenomena. The answer is that I haven't, but after reading innumerable books on the subject neither, I think, has anyone else. In many of these stories the reader can probably think of an explanation. Was the disappearing person on the road a poacher who deliberately dropped out of sight? Was the sighting of a deceased person a case of mistaken identity? But here and there are stories which are clearly told, obviously by an intelligent and down-to-earth person, for which there are no rational explanations.

Some anecdotes, for example, Michael Beard's story from Worcester, seem to infer some kind of telepathic link. Some stories suggest that a few people are able to pick up events which have happened or people who have lived in the past. What is surprising is the number of people experiencing some kind of poltergeist activity. As Barrie Roberts (writer and lecturer) says, 'The phenomenon occurs in every land and is documented back to the beginning of history' yet, even as the millennium approaches, we are still no nearer to finding the cause. We know a few facts, for example, that it seems attracted by certain people, usually a young person, often female and sometimes under stress or ill. However, this is not always so. In *Haunted Worcestershire*, in 'The man who caught a ghost' there was a poltergeist-type narrative where both people in the house were very elderly.

Over the years I have compiled a list of the phenomena associated with poltergeists. These are:

electrical disturbances with lights, tv, radio, telephone, etc;
problems with water supply eg ice suddenly appearing or water tasting strange;
inanimate objects disappearing, often for months, then usually reappearing in a strange place;
inanimate objects moving;
phantom footsteps;
strange noises for no reason, ranging from rustlings to loud explosions;
moving dark shadows, often in human form, occasionally manifesting themselves as real people.

I find that those who experience these phenomena often admit to be being slightly psychic, for example, they often know who is on the other end of the telephone before they answer it.

I hope that every one will enjoy these anecdotes and - most important - remember to telephone me on 01527 542516 if they have a ghost story which they can share. Anonymity is guaranteed if requested.

The 14th century Guesten Hall roof at Worcester cathedral before it
was dismantled in the 1860's, now at Avoncroft Museum of
Buildings, Stoke Heath, Bromsgrove, Worcester.
Courtesy Avoncroft Museum

WORCESTERSHIRE TOWNS

WORCESTERSHIRE

uring the civil war of 1642-1646, a Parliamentary soldier stationed in Worcester wrote to his home in London:

Worcestershire is a pleasant, fruitful and rich county, abounding in corn, woods, pastures, hills and valleys, every hedge and highway beset with fruit.

Four hundred years later, despite a population explosion and the industrial revolution, Worcestershire is still a pleasant, fruitful and lush county. The mighty river Severn traverses the entire length of the county from north to south and its tributary, the Avon, waters the south-east portion. West of Worcester is the river Teme and the river Stour is to the north. To the north west, the Malvern Hills rise to 1,400 feet, in the South East is Bredon Hill and in the north and north-east are the Clent and Lickey Hills. The blossom routes of the Evesham plain are one of the delights of England. On its northern edge Worcestershire has had exciting industrial successes - nails in Bromsgrove, needles in Redditch, carpets in Kidderminster.

Worcestershire is rich in produce and products - and rich in history. In medieval times, Worcester was one of the most important cities in England. When rivers were usually easier to travel along than roads, it stood on the junction of two important rivers, the Severn and the Teme. The castle towered high above the city and helped to guard England against invasions of the Welsh. Since recorded history began there has scarcely been a war or an invasion in which Worcestershire has not been heavily involved. The British Camp on the Malvern Hills was a British stronghold in the battle against the Romans. In the time of the crusades, many a soldier went off to war, such as Sir John Attewood of Wolverley. There was the battle of Evesham in 1265, where brave Simon de Montfort laid the foundations of democracy. No county was involved in the civil war of 1642/6 more than Worcestershire. The Gunpowder Plot was hatched in Worcestershire and it was to this county that the conspirators fled when their plot failed.

Over and over again Worcester city has been reduced to ruins. The Britons of Worcester were driven out by the Saxon king, Caelwin. The city was sacked again by the Danish king, Hardecanute when the citizens refused to pay taxes and killed his tax collector. In the wars between King Stephen and Queen Matilda, the city was sacked twice, once by each side. The Earl of

Worcester, Waleran, was a friend of King Stephen's. While he was away, Matilda's men arrived and burned the city to the ground. Earl Waleran was furious when he returned and set fire to some of Matilda's friends houses to retaliate. Then Waleran changed sides and decided to support Matilda instead. He shut himself up in his great castle in the heart of Worcester. Stephen decided to punish Waleran for changing sides, so Worcester was sacked again. The Welsh and the English have fought ever since Saxon times, and Worcester was plundered by the Welsh prince, Owen Glendower in 1405.

Worcester unfortunately backed the wrong side during the Civil War of 1642/6 and supported Charles I. After the battle of Worcester in 1651 those houses which were left standing were looted by the Parliamentarians. The latter were hated so much that when the new Guildhall was built, the townsfolk placed great statues of Charles I and Charles II on each side of the main door and above they carved an ugly little head, nailed by its ears, said to be the head of Oliver Cromwell.

Worcester Cathedral

In the days when Bishops were as important as kings, and the church governed day to day living, Worcester was a great religious centre. The Domesday Book records three other churches, St Andrew's, St Helen's and St Martin's, as well as the Cathedral. The city was filled with pilgrims visiting the shrines of Saint Oswald (who rebuilt the cathedral in about 961) and Saint Wulstan (who again rebuilt in about 1084). The Greyfriars had their house east of Friar Street and the Blackfriars settled by Broad street and Angel Lane. (See *Haunted Worcestershire*).

King John (1167-1216) asked to be buried at Worcester and his tomb is still there, although it has been moved from its original position between Saint Oswald and Saint Wulstan. The King hoped to slip into heaven unnoticed between the two saints. It is said that he died from eating a poisoned pear at an Abbey in Lincolnshire. The culprit is not known but it was observed that he had his eye on the Abbot's sister.

The darling of all England, Prince Arthur, was buried in the Cathedral in 1502. The richly carved chantry chapel over his tomb still adorns the eastern end. He was the eldest son of Henry VII, a sickly boy who was often brought to Malvern to breathe the pure air of the Malvern Hills. His father gave him Ludlow Castle and a house at Tickenhill, near Bewdley. He lived there with his young Spanish bride, Catherine of Aragon, and the happy young couple won the hearts of Worcestershire folk. When he died at sixteen the entire funeral route from Ludlow Castle to Worcester was lined with weeping figures. At the height of the funeral service a boy wearing the dead prince's armour and riding his horse, rode through the doors of the Cathedral, up the stone-vaulted nave and so to the Choir, where he dismounted. Had Arthur lived, Henry VIII would not have been king and the whole history of England would be different.

Miserrimus

A less flamboyant tomb lies just beyond the south door. If you look down at the floor just before you enter the gift shop in Worcester Cathedral you will see a large flagstone bearing the one word MISERRIMUS. The stone is at the bottom of a short flight of steps; at the top of these steps is the south door, known as the Miserrimus door. The Miserrimus stone is well-known and inspired Wordsworth's sonnet of the same name.

The locals say that on no account must you step on this stone because you will invoke the ghost of Thomas Morris. He was vicar of Claines and a minor canon of Worcester Cathedral. In 1689 he refused to take the oath of supremacy to King William and Queen Mary and consequently never rose through the ranks. He asked to be buried at the foot of these steps with the one word on his tombstone. He said that he had been walked over all his life and he would be walked over in death.

John, an ex-policeman, states:

It's well-known that under no circumstances are you to tread on the Miserrimus stone as this will invoke the ghost. Something from the past must have happened a number of times to make people believe this.

I joined the police force in Worcester in 1962 and worked that area for two years. If you were new you were put on a quiet beat which included Worcester Cathedral. We had to inspect the Cathedral twice each night, at one am and after our break, which was from two to six am. It was a very eerie experience. You had to go into College Green, unlock the gate and go into an unlit tunnel which led into a cloister. You then unlocked another door to find there were steps down directly onto the Miserrimus stone. From there you would go into the cathedral. You were totally without lights, you only had your torch and you had to feel your way across to the gift shop to find the light switches. When you opened the cathedral door you would see this green eye looking at you - central heating was provided by the old iron furnaces with a green glass inspection window in the top, there was one opposite the door as you went in. You would switch the lights on and turn round and as soon as you did so you would find some white marble fingers nearly up your nose from a white marble statue leaning forward with fingers raised. Both the gift shop and the statue have now been moved.

The Miserrimus door of Worcester Cathedral (next to the gift shop) with the Miserrimus stone at the foot of the steps.

Some of the old hands had worked the area for 20 odd years and they made sure that you knew the story of the Miserrimus ghost before you set out on your beat. Then sometimes they would hang a cassock over the door so that as you opened the door this black thing would come floating down on you.

Among those who have seen the Miserrimus ghost is Albert Price, who unfortunately passed away in 1995. He was a verger for over 50 years and used to recount the tale of how he saw the Miserrimus apparition in the 1920's. An elderly gentleman who has lived in Worcester all his life says:

I will tell you a story which you will not believe, but this is as true as I am standing here. I was 17 in 1934 and I was sitting on a bench with my girlfriend under the south west wall of the ruins of Gueston Hall. I expect the bench is still there, by the riverside. I was a smoker at that time and I remember blowing out three smoke rings sidewards. It was a brilliant moonlit night and as I looked up, I saw what I took to be an old dear looking out from a window. Three things struck me: first, who was she, second, what was she doing there and third, how did she manage to hang like that from that narrow window? I didn't say anything and away we went.

I was working at a shop in Broad Street and one morning soon afterwards I decided to go to Astons, the wholesale wood yard, to get myself a bit of cheap wood. I jumped on my bike and went along the quay side, and on the way I thought, 'I'll go and have a look and see if that old dear is still there'. When I saw the building in daylight and had a look at it from the rear, my flesh ran cold. Nobody had been up there for years. It was a straight drop to the ground and, as well, it was thickly encrusted with moss.

I can describe the person even now. I had first taken it to be an old lady but on looking back, I am sure that it was a monk. He was aged about fifty and wearing a rough type of garment with a square neck. He had shoulder length hair and a fringe. I saw him so clearly I could even see one rotten tooth in his upper jaw. He had his head on one side and was smiling down at me but plainly, the eyes told me everything - they had a kind but disapproving look.

I can tell you that, without a doubt, there is definitely a ghost in the cathedral grounds.

Gueston Hall was built between the Cathedral and the river Severn in about 1320, to accommodate important visitors. The wealth and influence of the church was then at its height. It was an exceptionally fine building but only the roof has survived. In 1862, the roof was moved to Holy Trinity Church, Shrubhill, but when this church was demolished in 1969 and 1970, the roof was moved to Avoncroft, where it has been re-erected.

The dark lady of the Commandery

On the other side of the road to the Cathedral but fifty yards or so towards the direction of the M5 is one of Worcester's pride and joys - the Commandery. It was founded by Saint Wulstan in 1085 as a hospital and at that time was just outside the town walls. The present half-timbered building, with its impressive great hall, is mostly fifteenth century. It is called the Commandery because, from the late thirteenth century, the masters of the hospital called themselves 'commanders'. The Commandery is the best remaining relic of the battle of Worcester, when some of the thousands of wounded were taken here. Among them was the Duke of Hamilton whose blood remained on a board on the ground floor until recent years. He was shot in the leg and while three surgeons were arguing as to his method of treatment, he died.

Perhaps it is the Duke of Hamilton whose dark shadow has surprised various members of staff down the years. However, in many cases this has taken a female form, as reported in the *Berrow's Worcester Journal* of 16 February 1996. Gary Bills writes:

> In 1936, Henry Badham, of Astwood Road, rented rooms in the Sidbury property, long before it was a museum, and said he was "always uncomfortable" in the presence of shadows.
>
> One evening, as he returned home up the Commandery drive to his wife and child, the unease took shape in the form of a dark grey female figure, moving towards him in the moonlight, before swinging right to accommodation then rented by a well-known Worcester artist, called Miss Davies.
>
> Mr Badham said: "When I spoke to Miss Davies in the morning, she said she had not been out the previous evening, nor had anyone called." ... The information seemed to confirm the authenticity of a photograph taken by an unknown member of the public several years ago in the Commandery garden.
>
> The picture, which has since disappeared, was of a grey female figure - something not visible when the shutter clicked.

Tears at St Helen's

One of the three churches mentioned in the Domesday book was St Helen's in the High Street which has undergone a wonderful conversion into the County Record office. Various unusual happenings have been reported there, and Tony Wherry, the County Archivist confirms that:

> there a number of stories concerning ghosts at St Helen's, the oldest of which is, of course, the story concerning the sound of the little girl crying.

Not a happy home-coming

Hylton Road runs alongside the River Severn and is almost inaccessible in times of heavy flooding. This is where the huge offices of the various Worcester journals and BBC Hereford and Worcester Radio are situated. The next interesting little story by Michael J Beard was originally entered for the Ghost Story competition organised by BBC Hereford and Worcester Radio in 1996.

I was asleep. It was sometime between two am and three am. "They" say that this is the body's time of least resistance, and can produce statistics to prove it. It was at this time in the early hours that my wife had been rushed into hospital with a brain haemorrhage. The hospital visits were very traumatic, but my wife was thankfully oblivious to her plight, as she lay unconscious awaiting the decision as to whether she was to be operated on. After waiting a week, she was rushed to the Radcliffe Infirmary, Oxford, where she receive a life-saving operation. She was very brave, appearing to be unaware of the grotesque swelling to her head, heavily swathed in bandages.

I awoke with a start. Something or someone was in the room with me. I was alone in bed. We had single beds and as I sat up and looked around me, there, in my wife's bed, was the outline of a person. As my eyes grew accustomed to the darkness I could make out the figure of my wife, her head heavily bandaged, sitting up in bed and watching me. I was terrified. I crawled slowly out of bed. With my back pressed against the wall I edged my way out of the bedroom into the hall as her dark eyes followed me. My legs wanted to run. My brain said just be calm; between the two I remained motionless. Unable to run, unable to reason. Gradually wild thoughts rushed into my mind. Why should the ghost of my wife visit me? Surely she was not dead. People let you know immediately when someone dies, don't they? We had a telephone. Would it ring? Was this a spiritual message to prepare me for the worst?

I don't know how long I remained in a semi-catonic state, but eventually common sense prevailed. If my wife was visiting me in some spiritual form, then surely she would mean me no harm. I slowly crept back into the bedroom. Nothing. No sign of a ghost. Strangely, I slept well for the rest of the night, and in the light of day I was able to talk myself out of any lingering fears of what could not possibly have happened. Or could it? My wife made a slow recovery, and eventually returned home to us. Her memory was damaged. After some five years she began to remember random incidents, small facts regarding her illness. When tested, she could repeat checkable facts about the hospital ward, the doctor's names, and odd little unimportant details. Her memory was beginning to recall small snapshots of her experiences in hospital.

During one of the rehabilitation sessions we had a conversation about a TV programme on out-of-body experiences. She revealed to me that during her first days at Oxford, she had had an out-of-body experience. In this she rose above the bed and looked down at herself lying there. It emerged that the times of her "experience" and my "visit" were the same.

So there is my ghost story. No shrieking Banshee, or howling Werewolf. No Dracula rising from the grave. These well-known ghouls are missing from my tale, because my story is true!

Worcester Cathedral

Glad to move house
Barbourne

If you follow the A38 through Worcester going north you arrive at Barbourne. The area was built mainly in 1865 as a distinct little town but it has now been swallowed up by the outskirts of Worcester. In 1949 Brenda Hopkins* and her husband were sharing a little house here with two elderly aunts.

They both wore dark, drab clothes with skirts down to their ankles and they both had grey hair in a bun. One of them was shorter than the other and quite round, the other was skinny. They were both in their eighties and I hadn't been there long when one of them died, then the other. A little later I had my first baby.

During the school holidays my twelve-year old niece came to spend the afternoon with me and to see the new baby. We were getting the tea ready and she was sitting at the table, pouring the tea when I looked up and, just for a second, I caught a fleeting glimpse of a dark figure the same size and shape as the thin aunt. I noticed my niece catch her breath, so I said, 'What's the matter?'. She told me that she thought she had seen Aunty Mary standing in front of the cellar door. I didn't tell her what I had seen. I said, 'You must have imagined it!'. What I saw was just a wispy image, nothing solid, and it all happened so quickly that if it hadn't been for my niece remarking on it I would have discounted it.

I was quite shaken and after that one or two things happened which really frightened me. I used to put some flowers in the house occasionally and twice I found them on the floor. At one time the vase was smashed and on another morning the flowers were out of vase and scattered over the floor. I was so unnerved that I mentioned it to the next door neighbours who had lived next door to my aunts all their lives. They said, 'Oh well, of course, these old ladies hated flowers in the house. When you used to bring flowers to them before you were married (which I did quite frequently) they always used to give them to me the next day.

I was terrified, and to make matters worse there was a penny in the slot electric meter which was down the cellar. Usually I managed to find enough pennies to ensure the slot meter was 'well fed' but there were occasions when the penny supply ran out. Whenever the lights went out whilst my husband was at work, I would not remain in the house but I used to walk up and down the road with the pram waiting for my husband to come home, rather than go down the cellar in the dark.

My husband told me that I was imagining it and so I didn't say too much more. However, one night we had some visitors and I went into the next room and left my husband talking to them. I had mentioned the flowers and I heard my husband say, 'Of course, I always tell her that she is imagining it but in fact, I was smoking a cigar one Saturday with my back to the fire and I myself saw a figure just for a second'. I burst into the room and said, 'I heard what you said!'.

The everlasting brawl
Ombersley Road

It's a sobering thought that a domestic argument could leave an impression on time. When she was a child Joan Bond lived on the Ombersley Road, north of Barbourne, and when an aunt came to stay ...

... my father moved into the little back bedroom. When he came down in the morning he said that the things in his bedroom had started whizzing round during the night, and when he sat up in bed he could see this young couple having a terrible row. They were throwing plates and all kinds of things at each other. We told a neighbour and she said that the poeple who lived there before us had had the same experience. My father refused to go into the back bedroom again and he insisted on selling the house and moving.

BROMSGROVE

romsgrove was once the nail-making capital of the world. By 1841, four thousand million nails were made every year in and around Bromsgrove. Working conditions were the worst and the lowest. Nail-making took place in small sheds or shops attached to houses, often only ten feet by nine feet. Despite the fierce heat of the forges, there was no ventilation except for the door. Children as young as seven worked in these conditions. Their wages were a pittance and the whole family had to work long hours in order to survive.

One organisation which tried to help the nailers was the Chartrists, a political movement which began in London in about 1838. It agitated for six major reforms such as votes for all and payment for members of parliament. National riots broke out in 1842 and 1848, and petitions with thousands of signatures were presented to parliament three times, in 1839, 1842 and 1848. Feargus O'Connor, a member of parliament, became leader. He created the National Land Company, where the ordinary working man would buy shares at one shilling each and when he had saved twenty-six shillings he would be eligible for a ballot where he would receive £15 for stock with three acres of land and a cottage at £5 a year rent.

In order to help the nailers he bought several acres at Dodford, just outside Bromsgrove, on the western side of the junction of the M5 and M42. There he established a village of about forty cottages, most of which are still there. Unfortunately, the scheme ended in disaster. Feargus often paid too high a price for land then mortgaged it in order to buy other areas. The tenants had no idea how to cultivate the land and three acres was insufficient to sustain a family. The National Land Company was wound up in 1848 and thousands of workers, including nailers, lost their precious shillings. Many of the cottages at Dodford were sold to the more affluent classes instead of nailers. Most of the nailers who were settled there gave up after a few miserable winters and returned to nailing.

A phantom fire
Fairfield

On the north-eastern tip of Dodford is Fairfield, a border village between the nail-making of Bromsgrove and the glass-making of Stourbridge. Fairfield

Court still exists, where those who broke the strict laws of Feckenham Forest were imprisoned and tried. Many were hung on the nearby gallows.

Les Smith was a passenger in a car on the A491 in the late 1970's, returning to Stourbridge from Bromsgrove.

It was one o'clock in the morning, my colleague and I had been out on business and we were absolutely sober. The petrol crisis was round about that time so there was no other traffic on the road. We were driving from the roundabout which I think is called Fairfield island (where the dual carriageway begins), just going past Bell End, when I realised that I could see a fire. As we got closer I saw that it was between the Bell Hotel and what is now a petrol station, although I don't think the garage had been built then. An old Elizabethan-style house standing right next to the road, if not on the road itself, had been almost completely consumed by fire. The strange thing was, that although the flames were going twenty or thirty feet above it, the framework of the house was still intact and was not collapsing at all. There was no crackling or any noise of any kind, and no smell of burning.

I said to my friend, 'Shall we stop?' and he replied, 'It will be in the newspapers in the morning' so he must have seen it as well. I looked in the papers the next day but I couldn't find out any more about it.

This has puzzled me ever since. I have since driven past the spot several times and there is an old house there but it is much further back than the one I saw. Was it a real house on fire? Did I see a house-burning re-enacted? Has anybody else seen it or can anyone thrown any light on this?

The mighty hunter
Lydiate Ash

To the east of Fairfield is the large Lydiate Ash island, where the M5 joins the Birmingham and Stourbridge roads.

Ann Payton says that although this happened twenty-two years ago now (1975), it is as vivid in her mind now as it was then.

I was driving back from Bromsgrove towards the Lydiate Ash island at one o'clock in the morning. My boyfriend lived in Bromsgrove and I lived in Woolaston. We had had a nice evening out, we had been to a cinema and then we'd sat in a pub car park for a bit of courting.

I was going down towards the island - you get the houses then there is a straight bit of road. The area was well-lit by the street lights. It was a quiet night, there was no traffic or anything at all about. I was nice and relaxed, I like to think while I'm driving. Then suddenly, a man on a horse appeared from nowhere and came directly across in front of me. If I had been driving fast I would have hit them. I looked in my mirror, but of course the road was empty, so I stopped in the middle of the road. I thought, 'I'm not seeing this!', I shut my eyes and opened them and they were still there. I stopped and watched them. They were a very proud pair, the horse was white and was holding its head high, like a stallion. The rider was more or less in silhouette, very upright and wearing dark clothing. I couldn't see his face, the area where his face should have been was blurred. He was tallish with a pointed hat, an old-fashioned riding cape and he had long boots. He and his horse went floating across the road. On the left hand side there was, at that time, a pull-in car park, a low hedge, a stretch of grass and another hedge. I sat there in the car and watched them float through both hedges before they disappeared.

I was just shocked. I sat there and I thought, 'How wonderful!'. When I got home I phoned my boyfriend, who is now my husband, and told him what I had seen. He said I must have been dreaming (actually, he said, 'You silly b...'). But whatever he said, I knew exactly what I had seen.

Ann could have seen any one of a whole series of legendary horses and riders. A mighty hunter, Callow, once lived in and around Feckenham Forest and is still supposed to haunt the area. His name lives on in Callow Hill (Redditch), Callow's Leap (Alfrick), and Callow's Grave (Tenbury).

Then there's the legendary Harry-Ca-Nab who haunts the nearby Lickey Hills. He was probably a poacher six hundred years ago in Feckenham Forest. Because of his offences on earth, he was consigned to hell at his death, where he became the devil's huntsmen. Tradition says that he rides a winged horse or a wild bull.

Perhaps the most likely is Sir Peter Corbet as the first two are usually supposed to be accompanied by their hounds. He lived at the original Harvington Hall and died about 1300.

A local legend tells of an underground passage that ran from Harvington Hall to Dunclent. Near to the hall a tunnel branched off and ended at a pit where the Hall's savage hounds were confined. One night, the hounds would not settle and when the huntsman investigated he heard voices and he fetched Sir Peter. They both heard an amorous conversation between Sir Peter's daughter and her sweetheart from Wolverley, in which they arranged to meet the following night. Sir Peter considered the man to be an unsuitable husband for his daughter, so next night, at the appointed hour of their meeting, he locked his daughter in her room and let the hounds loose. All that was left of the young man were his hands and his feet in his boots. On hearing the news, Sir Peter's daughter threw herself into the pool next to Harvington Hall and drowned. In his grief and remorse, Sir Peter hanged all the dogs and threw their bodies into the pool, which is still known as Gallow's Pool. For these terrible acts his ghost is condemned to eternal hunting throughout the night.

Return of the matriarch
Catshill

Across the motorway from Fairfield is Catshill. Its claim to fame is that the Gunpowder plotters galloped through here on 7th November, 1605. Despite being caught in the triangle between the M42 and the M5, this is a pleasant little village, where the old exists side by side with new housing. Anne Guest lives here in one of the new flats.

> There are eight flats here. They are really for elderly people but I was made homeless seven years ago and that's how I came to live here. I'm the youngest person in the flats. Among the residents at that time were two friends, a ninety-year old and a Welsh lady who was ninety-two years old. The Welsh lady lived on the ground floor and was a real matriarch. Whatever she said, went. Two years ago she died and somebody else moved into her flat.
>
> The ground floor flats have some security doors that can only be opened with the resident's security key. Some of the residents found this a bit of a nuisance and so they wedged the door open with a block of wood. The result was that there were a few thefts and the practice was stopped.

One day this summer I was in the garden when I heard this little Welsh voice say, 'I am sorry ladies, you cannot have this door open! I'm not having this door open!'. I looked up and there was the Welsh lady. I said to myself, 'I thought that lady had died, I must have got it wrong'. So I asked around and yes, she had died, and no, she hadn't got a twin or a sister who looked like her, in fact she had no relatives. I said, 'But I have just seen her at this back door!'. Anyway, I forgot all about it.

About two weeks ago, that would be the 7th September, I saw this Welsh lady scurrying across the road, between me and some garages. I thought, 'Oh Blimey, she's going next door' - this was where her friend lived. When I think about it now I recall that she was going much too fast for a little old lady. She sort of floated across the road. Anyway, her friend died that night. I wondered if she had called for her.

The unwelcome visitor
Marlbrook

The road through Catshill meanders on to the Lickey Hills. On either side of this road, just as it leaves Catshill, is Marlbrook, which is where Susan* and her husband, David* live.

Our house is a modern, three-bedroomed semi, built in the 1920's. My husband and I bought the house in about 1992.

The house is subject to power cuts. It's only our house that has the cuts, the neighbours don't have any. When I arrive home everything starts flashing, either the video or the alarm or the microwave. The strange thing is, they all show different times when they flash. The central heating clock keeps giving the wrong times.

One Saturday morning I was going round doing bits and pieces and David was in the back room with the door closed. Suddenly, the door opened and he felt as if someone was standing behind him. When he turned round, no-one was there. He is a very sensible, down-to-earth person but it was a while before he went back in there. Another time, he left the bathroom door open and he swore that he saw somebody walk past and go downstairs.

I often hear someone go up the stairs - definite footsteps, a man's heavy tread, quite loud as if he is walking on bare floorboards. Our stairs are carpeted. I used to think I was the only one who could hear them, but one night, David and my dad went out together and I was sitting watching the television with my mum, when my mum said, 'Oh, they're back!' I said, 'That's strange, I didn't hear the front door go' and my mum remarked that she heard somebody walk up the stairs.

One evening, I was lying in bed on my own in the dark when the bedroom door was pushed open. Someone seemed to come into the room, walk round the side of my bed and sit on my bed. I distinctly felt the bed go down. Thinking it was David, I turned the light on but no-one was there.

The cats look up and watch. And the dog - suddenly his ears pick up and he gives a slight growl. I can't see anything and I have never worked out why he growls.

I sometimes wonder if all this is anything to do with the fact that the elderly couple who lived in the house before us died here; the husband died in the bedroom and the wife fell down the stairs and lay there for some time until she was found.

Emergency - A ghost!

There were once many tales circulating about the old Bromsgrove Hospital. The hospital itself was built for American ex-servicemen during the war; after the war it became a general hospital. However, most of the paranormal incidents concerned the red brick building on the Birmingham Road, (number 165A) which was built in 1836 as a workhouse and used as such until 1901.

It was while it was being used as offices by the local health authority that the entire terrified domestic staff gave in their notices. The final straw had been the domestic supervisor opening a broom cupboard at the top of the central stairs to see the ghost of an elderly man sitting there. A compromise was reached when the district manager said that if they stayed on, they need not begin work until nine o'clock in the morning, when the office staff would have arrived.

The old hospital has now been rebuilt and renamed the 'Princess of Wales Community Hospital'. Consequently, the following two stories about the old hospital can now be told.

A head nurse, now retired, tells the story of the ward which always seemed to have a wheelchair stuck in the middle, getting in everyone's way. She complained about this several times to the ward sister, who eventually confessed that the wheelchair seemed to be haunted. They would put it away, then a minute later it would reappear in the same place. The local vicar performed a blessing and, as far as the head nurse knew, from that time on the wheelchair remained put.

The narrator of the next anecdote went into Bromsgrove Hospital in the autumn of 1969/70 for a minor operation.

Late at night that same day I woke up and I could hear a nurse and a man talking quietly. I was not at all whoozy, my mind was quite alert. I was at the top end of the ward and down the other end, in the half darkness, I could just make out the silhouettes of two figures. My first reaction was, 'Oh, one of the nurses has brought her boyfriend in'. The man was wearing a uniform - I could just see his silver buttons as they caught the light - and the woman was in a white nurses' uniform. What struck me was the fact that her white cap was the old-fashioned type, not the half cup which nurses wear now, but one which came down to her shoulders and was gathered at the back of the neck. I reached out and pulled the light on but to my surprise, nobody was there.

One of the nurses came in and I asked, 'Is there anybody on the bottom of the ward?' She said that there wasn't anyone.

Them dry bones
Sidemoor

The built-up area to the west of the hospital is known as Sidemoor. It was once just a handful of cottages, surrounded by marshlands and fields. One of the earliest cotton mills started in Sidemoor in the middle ages, probably making cloth-covered buttons. Jane still lives there, and she says:

This happened in about 1976 when I would have been eight or nine years old but even now, if I hear a creak on the stairs, I just shut my eyes and don't look.

My family lived in an old terraced house in Sidemoor, Bromsgrove. The upstairs had an unusual layout because you had to go through my bedroom, which was on the left at the top of the stairs, to get to the bathroom. I was in the bathroom when I heard a creak on the stairs. My sister was three years older than me and she used to lie in wait then jump me so I thought this was my sister lying in wait. I looked up, the bathroom door was open and I could see through my bedroom to the door at the top of the stairs. The door was open as wide as it would go, it didn't open fully because my bed was behind it. Then I saw that a nun was standing there - I assumed it was a nun because she was all in black with a white band round her head.

She had her back to me as if she was going to go out of the room but then she moved her left arm across her body and put her left hand on the knob of the door, as if she was going to come in backwards. I saw that it was a skeleton hand. She turned her head and looked towards me and her face was that of a skull. I shut my eyes and screamed and screamed.

My sister came running up the stairs followed by my mother and they said that there was nobody there. My mum put it down to watching too much television but I know without any doubt that what I saw was real. It was in the afternoon when the light was good and there was a large window in my bedroom and one behind me in the bathroom.

After that experience I was afraid of being left alone. It wasn't nice knowing that you had something like that in the house.

I only saw the nun on that one occasion and I haven't seen anything strange before or since.

The haunted quarry
Rock Hill

Bromsgrove quarrymen and masons were well-known for their skills in the Middle Ages. They worked chiefly in sandstone, most of which came from Hill Top and Rock Hill. For centuries, the same areas of Bromsgrove were also quarried for sand and clay, with the result that, by the end of the nineteenth century, quarries were dotted all over Rock Hill and Hill Top.

It seems likely, from old maps and records, that the haunted quarry is a remnant of the largest quarry on Rock Hill, owned by J & A Braziers Ltd. The founder of the company was Jonathon Brazier (1827-1895), the son of a nailmaker. Jonathon developed a flourishing building company; many of the houses round and about were built by Brazier's, and by the time he died he was employing 150 men. The quarry is now little more than a grassy depression about thirty yards across, comprising a row of garages and a children's play area.

Sharon Bowen says that she found the following experience most disturbing, and she has taken several people back to the quarry at the same time of night to see if they could provide a rational explanation, but none has been forthcoming.

The haunted quarry, Rock Hill, Bromsgrove

I have lived for forty years and I have never seen a ghost - until recently. My attitude has always been, if I don't see one, then ghosts don't exist. This was a first for me and it was really frightening.

We had a friend and her children staying for the day at our house in the Hilltop Estate, Bromsgrove. She came from the next estate and, as she didn't leave until well past eleven o'clock at night, I said to her, 'I'll walk with you and take the dog'.

From where I live there are short cuts to the Worcester Road, and from there to the old quarry play area at Rock Hill. As I neared the quarry I could see that, a short distance further along, there was quite a commotion going on with a group of older teenagers. One of the girls was in floods of tears and hysterical. She was sobbing heavily and you could see that she had gone a funny colour. I knew three of the teenagers and they said, 'We have just seen something, we think it is a ghost' and they asked me to go with them to take a look to make sure it really was something strange. I think they wanted confirmation from a responsible adult. I didn't want to get involved, I said, 'I don't really want to' but they insisted with 'Come one, come on'. The hysterical girl stayed behind.

As I went up the road towards the quarry I immediately sensed a change in the atmosphere, then I stopped dead in my tracks. I saw a wooden fence, about five feet four inches in height, and leaning over the fence towards me were two black silhouettes or shadows. It all happened so quickly it's difficult to remember what I saw. I thought they were probably the other side of the fence, as below the head and shoulders was just a dark patch, but they may have been this side and faded out from the shoulders. They were very prominent and quite high above the fence, they had either very long legs, were standing on something or were floating. In the few seconds that I saw them, the one slowly raised an arm and put it round the shoulder of the other. They then moved closer together so that the two shadows almost merged. We could hear breathing but the strange thing was, we could only hear a rhythmic breathing out, and not in.

I didn't want to believe what I was seeing and I tried desperately to find an explanation for it. I wondered if it could have been the shadows of trees, as there were trees nearby, but this wasn't possible. On the far side of the fence was a street lamp and I looked to see if it could have been throwing a strange light in some way, but it wasn't. My dog's ears pricked up and when I went to move away, his ears were back. He was obviously very scared. Then I fled without realising that I was running.

(This incident occurred in June 1999, just before publication. A meeting with those involved had to be cancelled because of an outbreak of 'flu in the area).

Then shall the dust return
Charford

The next house is near to the old Roman road, a saltway, which runs from Droitwich over the Lickey Hills, touching the north-western edge of Charford.

Our first house was a bungalow near Bromsgrove, where we lived for many years. I had two daughters and we only had two bedrooms so we were a bit cramped. Then a friend of mine said that she knew of an elderly lady who was on her own in a three-bedroomed house and she wanted to move to be near her daughter. I refused to see the house because I didn't want to move but the family were keen, so an exchange was arranged and it all went through very quickly.

Because we hadn't had stairs before, I used to leave the landing light on for the children so that they didn't fall downstairs. I also left my bedroom door ajar. About a week after we moved in, I woke up with the feeling that somebody was standing by me. You know how it is when you have been ill and somebody has brought you a cup of tea, you're slow rousing yourself, well, it was like that. Then suddenly, in the half light I could see a man. I pushed my husband until he woke up and said, 'There's somebody in the house'. He went and looked round but nobody was there and he said I must have dreamed it. I saw this man so clearly I could describe him. He had a squarish-shaped face with a ruddy complexion, black curly hair, grey flannel trousers with braces and a heavy Oxford shirt without the collar. This happened again on two or three occasions. One night, he stood there and I saw him so clearly I couldn't understand why my husband couldn't see him. I used to say, 'There he is, there, look!', but my husband couldn't see anything.

The next time I saw him I was really quite frightened. I was standing on the landing, looking out of the window in broad daylight, holding my little white poodle in my arms, when I felt that somebody was standing behind me and I suddenly felt very cold. My poodle was growling and barking and she wet herself with fright.

By that time, we had been in the house about six or eight weeks. My next door neighbour had kept asking me to go round, so I shot downstairs, shoved the poodle into the little room and ran next door. I said to the lady next door, 'You keep asking me round and I've never been'. She said to me, 'You're as white as a sheet, whatever is the matter?' I said, 'Well, I can't really say' but she made me a cup of coffee and promised not to laugh. When I told her, she said, 'Oh, I'm so glad you've told me, I could hear you both walking round in the night'. She asked me to describe the man I had seen. She then told me that it sounded just like the previous occupant of the house who had died five years previously. She said that I shouldn't be afraid, he was a lovely man. After that, I was never really afraid as such.

By that time my one daughter was about thirteen or fourteen. She came back from visiting a friend and said, 'You know you always say that there is a ghost in this house. My friend says she wouldn't live in this house for anything as it's haunted'. Evidently the previous occupant had an adult daughter and, after he had passed away, if she went out with her friends and returned after eleven o'clock she used to stay with a friend rather than go home. She said that as she went up the stairs her father used to walk down past her.

I was still very sceptical about the identity of the ghost and I wanted to prove that the man I had seen was the previous occupant. A year or two later I bumped into the acquaintance through whom we had originally heard about the house going on the market. As we were walking together up the hill I said, 'Do me a favour, will you?' and I asked her to describe to me the previous occupant. She said that he was a big man with a ruddy face and black curly hair who worked out-of-doors. I said that it was important to me find out exactly how he was dressed and she said that he usually wore grey flannels and braces with one of those horrible Oxford shirts.

I knew then that it was this man that I had seen and after that I wasn't afraid. I told the vicar and he said that I was very fortunate - all these years he had been a minister and nothing like that had ever happened to him.

Then the apparition stopped appearing. Some time later I heard that the woman from whom we had bought the house had died. A thought suddenly struck me and I asked around to find out exactly when she had died. It was just about the same time that the man had stopped appearing.

It is my personal opinion that he was coming back to look for his wife. Then, when his wife went to join him, he stopped searching for her. My neighbour tells me that we have our bed in exactly the same position as the bed of the previous occupant.

The crying baby
Central Bromsgrove

Bromsgrove centre has more than its fair share of ghosts. Part of the front of Woolworths was once a house, and here a sickly child used to sit and watch the goings-on in the road outside, his ghost haunted the upper floor for several years. The Bromsgrove Messenger offices are said to be haunted by an old printer. Boots the Chemists stands on the site of a public house, the Green Dragon, which was haunted by a man who hanged himself in there. The original part of the Royal Mail office dates back to the 1700s; one of the Post Masters used to smoke a pipe with a distinctive type of tobacco and from time to time present-day workers still catch a whiff.

When Pat was first married in the 1960's she moved to a house close to the town centre:

Nearly every night, I used to hear a baby crying. At first, I didn't think much about it - I assumed it was a neighbour's child. I worked in the day so I was only at home in the evening and I didn't know any of the neighbours. A few months went by and I gradually got to know the people in the area. I discovered that there wasn't any child living nearby. I wasn't frightened, just curious.

I thought it might be my imagination so one evening I said to my husband, 'Can you hear anything?' and he answered, 'I can hear a baby crying'. When he went to work he asked about the people who had lived there previously. The house had been empty for some time before we moved in. The couple before us had had a little boy who had died of cancer when he was two years old. Although he had died in hospital, he had spent most of his final months at home.

The unfortunate lodger

*Sue's two teenage lads were living at home when her partner left her in 1998. That same year, Sue met *Miranda, a divorced student in her mid-twenties with a small boy. Miranda was having accommodation problems at the time and so Sue offered her a home. Miranda made a first class lodger, she was sensible, sweet-natured and conscientious, and the two women soon became firm friends. The two teenagers left home, one after the other, leaving Sue, Miranda and the boy in the house. However, Sue soon discovered that Miranda was not the ideal lodger she first thought. She says:

I have lived in this house for fifteen and a half years and nothing like this has ever happened before.

The telly keeps flicking on and off, I think it will blow soon. The video has stopped working completely. My stereo was an expensive one, it cost over £1,000, and now the tape deck has broken. The CD player doesn't work. We used to have three clock radio alarms, my two teenagers had one each and I had one. The alarm doesn't go off on now on any of them. I had had my clock radio for years. We borrowed a stereo from my friend's mother. As soon as Miranda touched it the drawer came open and wouldn't go back in. We had to stick sellotape across it to keep it in. I have had this two-bar electric fire for six or seven years but I rarely use it as we have central heating. Miranda moved in and, after about five months, one of the bars stopped working. Miranda has been here just a year and during that time every appliance in the house has broken.

I bought her a Karaoke for Christmas. Now the tape decks have gone. We thought the kids had been messing with it, they had been listening to tapes all day. They really had a good telling off over that.

As soon as she touches something, it goes wrong. She borrowed a computer from college and she had to take it back because it wouldn't save any of her work. I bought her a computer for a present. We set it up, then one day Miranda came to use it and it wouldn't work. I put it on top of the wardrobe and forgot about it. The other day I found it and it started working perfectly for me. Miranda started typing her college work in and immediately the tape got all chewed up.

Another thing is the bulbs. The number of light bulbs we use is unbelievable. We buy at least ten a month. The first week that she moved in all three light bulbs in the kitchen went. We bought three more and almost immediately, two of those went. The bathroom light has gone four times this year.

Other strange things happen. The water keeps tasting so funny that we have to throw our cups of tea away and make another. You fill the kettle up and the water runs out of the bottom but when you hold it up to the light you can't see a split at all.

Things are always going missing. A few days ago Miranda's bus pass was in that drawer, then it completely disappeared. For a couple of days she had to pay to get to college. We used to think it was the children but now we only have one small boy in the house. The tweezers and the scissors are always going missing. And the mugs! When Miranda moved here she brought a load of mugs and I already had a lot so we had a cupboard full. We're now down to about six. We haven't loaned them out and they haven't been broken so where are they? We have also lost tea-towels, hundreds of them. I had a drawer full and when Miranda came she bought the ones from her house. They have all disappeared and now we are down to our last three. And I have lost pants. I've always made sure I have plenty of decent underwear and now I'm down to about half-a-dozen pairs. Where have they gone? You don't wear other people's underwear. Do we have a phantom panty-nicker?

We have put sets of keys on the sideboard in the kitchen and they have gone. We have both seen them put there, yet they're missing. We have looked everywhere, then gone to the shops with another set of keys. When we come back we go into the kitchen and there are the keys, right in front of us, perhaps over the other side of the room. This happens more times than not.

I had a photograph which was very dear to me and it stood on my bedside table. Miranda also had on her bedside table a photograph which was very dear to her. Now, about the same time, both those photographs went missing. Wasn't that strange?

We buy two or three bags of sugar a week. I said to Miranda, we must be putting sugar down the drain. We buy bags and bags. The more we buy, the more it disappears! I bought myself a jar of a special marmalade and when I went to the cupboard a few days later the jar was almost empty. I was really annoyed. I couldn't understand it because no-one else in the house liked marmalade.

Often, when we go shopping, the till won't work. If I go shopping on my own, everything is fine, and if Miranda goes on her own, nothing happens, but if we go together, it's murder. Something always goes wrong at the checkout. I don't know why, but it's never our bill that goes wrong, it's the one in front of us.

Miranda was listening to this conversation, nodding her head and interrupting occasionally. At this point she joined in the conversation.

I feel as if I'm an accident waiting to happen. People think I'm clumsy but I'm not, it's just that everything goes wrong when I touch it, especially if I'm feeling down. I often wonder if it was something to do with my aunty. She died when she was only eighteen months old. It's just a coincidence that I happened to be born on her birthday. I have a photograph of her and if you compare it with a photo of me at that age you would think it was the same person.

Sue gets very angry with me sometimes. What particularly annoys her is if I cannot find something which Sue puts her hand on straight away. This happens over and over again, on a regular basis. I get the whole wardrobe out looking for an article of clothing, then Sue walks over to the wardrobe and puts her hand on it straight away. I know damn well I have searched properly. A few months ago I dropped a ring on the floor and I looked everywhere. I shook every shoe in my room. Then Sue came in and the ring dropped out of the first shoe that she shook.

23

I have strange dreams. There are two dreams that I have over and over again. In the first dream I am searching for my nan and after I have been to many different places, she allows me to find her. The second dream is that I see this person - she has her back to me - who is being approached by something evil and I need to help her.

Sometimes I have a dream and the next day everything happens as it did in my dream. I know what people are going to say and do because I saw it in my dream. Sometimes when I get on a bus I could swear black and blue that I have seen these people before and heard the same conversations. Last week, I dreamed that a particular student at college was telling another student that he had gone to see this particular play and it was involved with some tribal thing - a ritual. The next day I could not believe my ears when I heard his friend asking him if he had been to see such-and-such a play. The conversation went on exactly as I had dreamed it.

Occasionally I can hear this mumbling. I usually think it's Sue and I call out 'What is it?' but she hasn't said anything.

Sue likes to play practical jokes and sometimes she hides, then jumps out and shouts 'boo'. Nine times out of ten I can sense that she is hiding, although I can't hear or see her. At other times I feel that somebody is behind me, but when I turn round, there isn't anyone. Often I get a quick glimpse of someone out of the corner of my eye, it seems grey and I can see lines, like the line of an arm or the line of a headpiece coming round the face. My heart goes bumpetty bump.

Reluctantly, Sue confessed to an apparition of some kind in the house.

I had a friend staying here with two lads. They were up in their bedroom, having a drink and playing cards with some music. One of the lads was standing by the door and he said that he saw a ghost come out of the other bedroom, walk across the landing and go into our bedroom. He was so upset that he had to go home. On another occasion we had a fifteen year old girl staying with us and she was adamant that the ghost of a lady had visited her during the night.

I have lived here all this time and I have never seen, heard or experienced anything like that. I think it's significant that both these ghosts were seen during the last twelve months, while Miranda was staying here.

DROITWICH

roitwich is situated above large deposits of rock salt, formed millions of years ago. The brine was so strong that one gallon of brine, when evaporated, gave two-and-a-half pounds of salt. Droitwich is the oldest salt-producing centre in the country. Its history could have begun 6,000 years ago when prehistoric hunters were attracted to the area by the game visiting the salt springs. In its recorded history, two people stand out as having saved the fortunes of the town, the one is John Corbett, who developed Droitwich as a spa town (see *Haunted Worcestershire*), and the other is Saint Richard.

Saint Richard was born in Droitwich in 1197, reputedly at (what is now) the Raven Hotel. He went to Oxford but his estate was mismanaged so he returned to Droitwich to restore the family fortunes. This done, he resumed his studies at Oxford, Paris and Italy and France. In 1244 the Bishops elected him Bishop of Chichester. However, Henry III had wanted another member of the clergy to be Bishop and Richard was outlawed. His property was confiscated and an edict was issued, forbidding anyone to help him. The legend is that he became a hermit at Droitwich. Certainly he had nowhere to live and had to rely upon people giving him food and clothing. Finally, the Pope ordered the King to accept Richard or be excommunicated and so Richard became Bishop of Chichester in 1247.

The One-Stop Council Shop's so-called 'Devils Dolls'

Sometime during his early years as Bishop, Richard returned to Droitwich. The story is that he arrived to find that a terrible disaster had occurred. The brine springs had dried up which meant that Droitwich would be ruined. The superstitious townsfolk thought this was because they no longer followed certain heathen rituals. Richard arrived just as heathen dances were being performed. Horrified, he blessed the brine pit which, fortunately, began to flow. Sir Hugh Fromere, Lord of Crowle and senior bailiff cried out, "My Lord, you have saved the town, this day will never be forgotten in Droitwich". Richard died on 3rd April, 1253 and for hundreds of years the anniversary of his death was celebrated in Droitwich as a public holiday.

Four hundred years later the townsfolk of Droitwich, together with the rest of England, were still clinging to their old superstitions. The old Celtic and pre-Celtic beliefs that birds could somehow predict or affect our future, lingered on. Cocks were thought to avert evil or cure disease and were often buried in the foundation of buildings. As recently as the 1930's women would often wear a silver-mounted cock's foot as a brooch. When a store in the High Street, was redeveloped and refurbished in 1992, a cockerel's claw was found, carefully placed in the wall at the front of the building between the two floors. The proprietor asked for the claw to be left as it was obviously there to protect the house.

The discovery of two dolls during the redevelopment of the One-Stop Council Shop also in the High Street, caused great excitement in 1996. They were about ten inches tall, with lurid, painted faces, each wrapped in a muslin cloak. Although they were probably put there as a 'good luck' symbol, it was thought at first that they were images of real people made for witchcraft purposes. The witch would stick a pin into a certain area in the doll and this should inflict some pain or calamity in the same area of the actual person. They were therefore nicknamed 'the devil dolls' and the workmen removed them from the building.

Almost immediately, everything seemed to go wrong. A frightening explosion on the site heralded the terrible fact that a digger had ploughed through a power cable, cutting electricity from homes and shops. Then, to everyone's surprise, the foundations of a building even older than the fifteenth century Council Shop was found. Work was held up while this was investigated. Illness and bad weather delayed work still further. Finally, the contract was so far behind schedule that the workers were convinced that they were jinxed and threatened to down tools unless the dolls were returned to the Shop.

And there they remain, sitting smugly in a glass cabinet on the wall of the reception area.

A spectral spectacular
The Norbury Theatre

We may laugh at these old superstitions but it's surprising how many still exist today. People often refuse to walk under a ladder or throw spilt salt over their left shoulder. Theatre folk are a superstitious lot and there's a belief that the spirits of past actors visit the theatre in the form of butterflies. The Norbury Theatre, in Droitwich, is subject to the sudden appearance of exotic butterflies even in the cold weather. Every theatre has its ghost and

the Norbury is no exception, as Peter Mellors testifies:

Many people have asked me where the unusual name comes from. The theatre is on the site of Norbury House, home of a wealthy family of solicitors going back to the seventeenth century.

This old house, with its oak beams, deep cellars and large marble fireplaces, remained as part of the hotel complex when a new luxury hotel was built in 1936. Part of this building was developed into our theatre in 1962/63 and the old house was demolished. Friar Street is full of interesting buildings, over the road is the Old Cock Inn which incorporates bits of the old St Nicholas church, the priory church desecrated during the civil war. Norbury House itself was built on the site of the medieval priory. This house was pulled down and a second one built as a hotel in 1936 which has been developed into our theatre.

During the 1950's and early 1960's the Droitwich Theatre and Arts Division, of which I am a member, used to do a pantomime at the local wintergardens and cinema. However, the Council decided that they were going to close the cinema and develop the wintergardens so we were all wondering where we should put on our shows.

At that time, Norbury House was vacant and we were allowed to build and paint the pantomime scenery in there. One cold, frosty, foggy evening in late November I found myself working alone in the dining room, which is now the auditorium. Several friends should have been there but had failed to turn up, some were ill and it was much too cold to work there if you were not well. Only one or two spotlights were on and most of the house was in darkness. Suddenly, I heard the howling of a dog. The noise made me look up and I saw, peering in at one of the windows, a pale, misty face. It was very difficult to reach the windows as the gardens had been neglected and were overgrown with brambles. I put down my paintbrush and went to the window to investigate. A figure in a greyish-white cowl was moving slowly away, I saw it clearly and it looked quite real. Although it was a long time ago I can remember it precisely. I watched it for several seconds before it faded away. After that I packed up and went to join everyone else at rehearsals. When they saw me they said, 'My goodness, I didn't think it was as cold as all that!'. My hair must have been standing on end. A few days later I received the good news that Norbury House was to be let on lease and the lease was to be offered to the theatre group.

My wife was stage manager and she has had one or two strange experiences. The lights on stage can only be operated by a main switch off stage called a 'big breaker'. My wife arrived on stage in the twilight and suddenly the lights came on. Thinking that a stage hand had arrived and switched them on for her, she called, 'Thanks!'. A little later she realised that she was on her own in the place. She had a similar experience one Saturday evening about nine years later when she was down in the other part of the theatre.

More recently, I was in a different part of the building late one evening, working by a single light, when I suddenly felt an unusual chilling sensation and in the dimness I made out a figure disappearing through a closed doorway. Since we have converted Norbury House into a theatre other people have caught sight of this figure on one or two occasions.

The figure always seems to appear when we have a problem and it seems to settle them. The last time was some fifteen years ago, when we were having problems with our limited space backstage and to the stage 'wings'. This was when I last saw this figure, soon afterwards Wychavon District Council came to our assistance and built an extension to the stage and backstage areas. We have been experiencing problems at the theatre recently, well-reported in the local press. Perhaps our friendly ghost will come to our assistance this time.

The Wychbold apparition

In *Haunted Worcestershire*, published in December 1996, Paul Parsons tells of an apparition that he encountered just past the gatehouse to the Chateau

Impney in 1975. It was a dark, cold and windy night, with rain lashing down. Paul saw a man in his twenties 'wearing a great big dark coat almost down to the ground with the collar pulled right up'. Seventeen years later on an equally squally evening Barbara Middlemass saw a similar apparition a mile further on, not far from Webb's garden centre.

> One Autumn evening in about 1992 my husband and I were driving from our home near Droitwich to visit friends in Bromsgrove. It was about 7 o'clock and a miserable night - cold, dark and pouring with rain. My husband was driving and we were travelling at about 40 mph with another car a good distance ahead of us.
>
> We had just passed the caravan sales office at Wychbold when a man stepped off the side of the road in front of us. I yelled to my husband, "Watch that man!". I can see him now in my mind's eye. He was a mature man, thirty to forty years of age and very elegant looking, tall and thin in a long black coat - like a traditional highwayman's coat - which was open with the collar turned up. He was wearing a tall hat but no gloves and crossed the road in front of the car at an angle instead of going straight across. On the other side of the A38 road is a big tree with a farm gate beside it and he disappeared from my view through the gate.
>
> Although he was twenty or thirty yards in front of the car I could see him quite clearly, and I particularly remember his purposeful stride. I was not at all frightened because he looked so real, except for the fact that his legs appeared to be cut off above the ankles and it seemed as if his feet were covered in mist. My husband did not see him at all. When we arrived at our friends' house in Bromsgrove I explained to everyone what had happened. No-one laughed, but a large whisky was thought to be the order of the day. After all this time I still have a very clear picture of the man, and always look for him when passing the place where he appeared. Strangely enough I have never seen him again.

A Roman soldier helps with the stock-taking
Berryhill Industrial Estate

Considering that the Romans were in the Midlands for more than three hundred years, with a strong presence in Droitwich, we have remarkably few Roman ghosts. Fortunately we have one here from Robert Nicklin.

> I worked at this company on the Berryhill Estate, Droitwich, for ten years, from 1987 to 1997. When I first started, we used to do a stocktake twice a year which would take the whole day and the factory would be closed. Normally, the factory is very noisy but for the stock-take, the machines would all be turned off and the dead silence would be very creepy.
>
> We were still working at about nine-thirty or ten o'clock one night. There were just three of us, Nick Williams, myself and a third person in the office. Nick and I were sent to the other

end of the factory to do a recheck. We were walking up the factory when we both saw what I swear was a Roman soldier. It was very dark so I could only see a dark shape, but I could make out his shield, which was rectangular, about four feet long and two-and-a-half feet wide, and his helmet, which was a bit like a world war I German soldier's helmet with a point on top and a crest. I was sideways on to him and Nick was coming up from behind. This Roman soldier was walking in a straight line and you can't do that in a factory, the machines are in the way, so he was walking through the machines. I couldn't believe what I saw and thought someone must be playing a joke on us, so I said to my mate, 'You go round that way and I'll go round this. If somebody's still here, messing us about, we want to know who it is'.

We came together and it was obvious nobody was about. I looked at Nick and he looked at me and he said, 'Let's go'. I said, 'I'm not stopping here, I'm off down the office'.

I haven't seen anything before or since. We often meet up and we have a laugh over it. Nobody has been able to explain it. Somebody did tell me that there's an old Roman burial ground under the Berryhill estate.

Robert may well be correct. The Romans occupied Droitwich in the middle of the first century. The earliest natural springs were in the Vines Park area of the town (the other side of the Saltway from the car parks) and so this is where they settled. They built a large fort at Dodderhill and a luxurious villa by the Kidderminster Road. Between the two, in 'the old playground' in Vines Lane, was their burial ground which extended across several hundred yards. Part of the estate may therefore lie over the burial ground.

EVESHAM

here are now only a few remnants of the great Benedictine Abbey at Evesham, founded in 714 by Saint Egwin (see *Haunted Worcestershire*). All that remains of this magnificent abbey which was larger than Pershore or Tewkesbury, is the curtain wall and a barely recognisable fourteenth century entrance gateway. Abbot Lichfield's lovely bell tower has survived behind Evesham's two churches, so has the fifteenth century Almonry, where the Almoner lived whose duty it was to oversee the sick and needy. TheAlmonry has been converted into a fascinating museum.

Although the Abbey has almost disappeared, tales of scandals and shameful deeds have lived on down the centuries. Even the saintly Egwin seems to have been guilty of a misdemeanour or two. He had many enemies, partly because he spoke out strongly against various sins including adultery; consequently, he was accused of a number of crimes. He therefore decided to go to Rome to speak to the Pope. The story is told that before setting out he had his legs chained and padlocked, then he threw the key into the river Avon. When he reached Rome he told his followers to wait by the Tiber while he went to pray. While waiting, they decided to go fishing and caught a salmon. When the salmon was prepared for the evening meal the key was found inside the fish and Egwin was able to be released from his chains. The *Victoria County History* is of the opinion that Egwin made up the story himself.

Then there are all the forged documents. Letters from the Pope Constantine in 709 and 713 are clearly fakes. A charter exists from 710 stat-

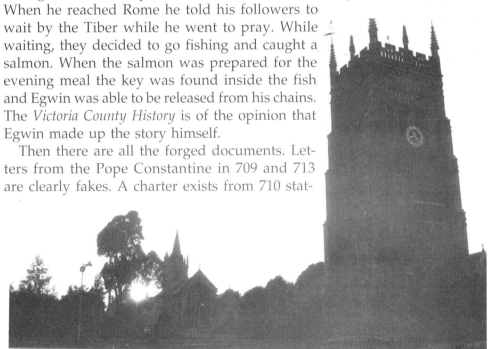

The Bell tower, built by the last Abbot of Evesham in the first half of the sixteenth century

All Saints is on the left, Saint Lawrence is on the right, both in the abbey precinct

ing that land was granted to the abbey in twelve places including Bidford, but, says the *Victoria County History*, this is 'evidently spurious'. So are the grants of Ethelbald of Mercia in 716 and 717.

There was a struggle for possession of the Abbey after Egwin died in 717 and one of the Abbots threw out the monks and installed his friends and colleagues. In 960 Bishop Oswald managed to get the monks reinstated but they were again ousted in 976 by a Mercian prince. Although he recanted on his deathbed the monks were unable to evict the occupants.

Somewhere between 1149 and 1159 Abbot William de Andeville attacked William Beauchamp's castle at Bengeworth. and destroyed it. These were the times of the civil wars of Stephen and Matilda, when anarchy, pillage and destruction ruled, and Abbots needed to be militarily competent as well as pious.

Then came the worst scandal of all. Abbot Roger Norreys 'wasted lands and revenue, stinting brethren on clothes and food while he enjoyed every luxury'. The monks had to beg for food instead of distributing it. They had to stay in the infirmary because they had no clothes and the *Victoria County History* reports that they could not say mass 'because they had no breeches'. The monks appealed to the Archbishop of Canterbury who came to Evesham to look into the matter but Abbot Norrey's bribed some monks to speak well of him. Bishop Manger also came to investigate but Abbot Norreys had obtained certain privileges for the monks which they would lose if he left, so they said nothing. He was finally deposed in 1213.

There seems to have been divine retribution because in 1207 the tower fell, fire broke out in 1217, in 1261 the tower was struck by lightning and it was wrecked by a storm in 1291. The abbey church and buildings were destroyed after the sixteenth century reformation.

Black Bridge

The abbey was was a thriving community when the battle of Evesham was fought outside its walls. The centre of Evesham, which includes the abbey, is built in a loop of the river Avon. In 1265, Simon de Montfort decided to rest his army in this loop, and await the arrival of his son with reinforcements. Simon climbed the abbey tower and saw an army approaching over Green Hill (on the northern side of the town) with his son's banners fluttering in the wind. It was a trick. His son had been defeated, his banners taken and the army was actually that of his enemy, Prince Edward. Simon was trapped in the loop of the river. He and another son were killed and it was reckoned that four thousand soldiers died that day. The worst fighting took place near the present railway station and when the bridge was built over the railway line the locals christened it, 'Black Bridge'.

A new member of the Vale of Evesham Historical Society tells this story:

Three weeks ago I moved into a lovely house near to Black Bridge. I didn't know anything about the history of the area but several times during the first week I experienced the sensation of things moving, out of the corner of my eye. It was so vivid that I was spinning round and looking to see who it was. Each time I saw something I experienced a definite tang, a sort of gingery smell.

My daughter came up from London the first weekend to see my house and as soon as she walked in she said, 'This house is haunted'. I said to her then, 'I will tell you something that I would never have mentioned' and I told her that several times I had glimpsed

Saint Lawrence's church from the Bell Tower arch.

something.

   Last Saturday, I met some friends and in the course of conversation one of them mentioned that the area was supposed to be haunted and that he, personally, had seen a shadowy figure on Black Bridge. I was intrigued because someone had told me a story about an apparition without me telling my story.

The Victorian lodgers

The family involved in this story are so afraid of the house being identified that they have told their story through a third party, Reg Ward, who says:

Some friends of mine lived in a house in Evesham which was only about ten years old and which had been built on land which had no special history, having contained nothing but a few derelict sheds. However, the ground there had once been swampy and we did wonder whether a drowning or some other misadventure had given rise to the most peculiar experiences they had there.

The whole family, comprising the parents and three children, the eldest in his mid-teens, regularly saw two apparitions. The one was a Victorian lady or someone dressed in a costume reminiscent of the turn of the century, and the other was a Victorian girl dressed in pink with a lot of petticoats. It is generally assumed that when apparitions put in an appearance they walk along the route that they took in life, but these particular ghosts used to go up and down the stairs! On one occasion, as the family went from room to room, the little Victorian girl followed them!

The Victorian lady often appeared in the eldest son's bedroom. Once he woke up and found her bending over him. He found her such a nuisance that he threatened to leave home.

One morning, the wife stood in the window waving goodbye to her husband, who said later that there was a tall white shape standing behind her. The wife's father had recently passed away and they assumed that he was paying them a final visit. The other ghosts were complete strangers.

They had a slight poltergeist. The wife was sitting downstairs late one evening when there came a most almighty crash from upstairs. She rushed upstairs to see what had happened but nothing was out of place.

Although the house was modern it always felt cold and clammy, even when the central heating was turned on full.

There was nothing malevolent in the apparitions but in the end their frequent appearances got the family down, so much so that they moved house. They did not tell the buyers that the house was haunted but have heard through mutual friends that the present occupants have seen nothing.

The harbinger of death

The following story is told by a retired gentleman who was born and bred in a little village between Evesham and Stratford. The house was bought by his mother when it was new in 1929.

For many years, I lived in a haunted house. Believe me, if you are sceptical beforehand, you are not sceptical after something strange has happened to you.

Imagine the scene. In room A, my mother's grandmother is dying. She is being nursed by my grandmother, my mother's mother. My mother and father are standing at the top of B and they are chatting to another person. They all notice a figure go from A, across the bottom of B and out through the other door and up the stairs between room B and C.

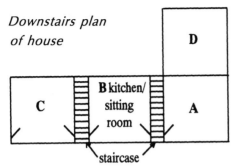

Downstairs plan of house

They only casually glance at the figure and think it is my grandmother passing from room to room in her dressing gown. A short time later, to their surprise, grandmother passes from A to B. They say to her, 'How did you get back again? We just saw you go the other way in your dressing gown!'. My grandmother replies, 'I would have liked the opportunity. I have not had my clothes off for the last 24 hours!'. Who went up the stairs?

Note: you cannot get from A to B unless you retrace your steps.

The next incident occurs when I am about two years old. My mother and father are in the bedroom which is above D. Therefore to get from these stairs (between room B and C) to their bedroom you have to go along a long landing. I am in the room close to the top of the stairs. My mother wakes up, hears footsteps and calls my name. My father says, 'Hush, those are not a child's footsteps, they are too heavy. I have heard them go along the landing twice'. At that point the footsteps come back and the bedroom door slowly begins to open. When my parents told me this story, I asked them, 'What happened next?'. Their answer was, 'We don't know, we both had our heads down under the bedclothes!'.

When I was small I appeared to have got into the habit that I would go downstairs after I had been put to bed, saying that I wanted some supper or a glass of water. Father gets fed up with this and so, one night, when my mother has gone out and my father is sitting in his chair in room B, footsteps come down the stairs and he thinks, 'I'm going to stop the young man's capers'. The door handle turns and he sits there, waiting to pounce, but nothing happens. The dog bristles up and backs slowly under father's chair. Eventually he opens the door but nobody is there and I am fast asleep in bed.

On another occasion my father comes home late with a friend of ours. I think they had both been down to the local, and they sit there talking. Finally, the friend gets up, picks up the cat says, 'Come on Bob, we will all go out together'. He goes out from room B to the outside on the far left. He reappeared a moment or two later as white as a sheet and saying, I quote, 'Who's been playing silly b...'s? I got to that door and something pushed me to one side. Then the door was open and shut in my face!'. We ask him what has happened to the cat and he said that it went out like a rocket before the door closed.

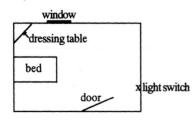

Layout of bedroom

We now come to early November 1951. I am just 20 years of age and I am reading in bed. I suddenly look at the clock on the dressing table. It is midnight and the next morning I have to be at work by 7 o'clock. I get out of bed on the dressing table side and walk round the bottom of the bed to the light switch. I put out the light and everything goes dark (except for the window which is not absolutely black) so that my eyes have not retained an image. I am about to get into bed when I remember that I have been playing with the clock and I have not set the alarm hand. There is only one thing for it - I have to get out of bed and perform this task. I now go back to put out the light. As I turn to the wall which is opposite the bottom of the bed on the right hand side I see that it is glowing pink. I think it must be some queer light a car has on, so I look at the window but no, the window is dark. I come round the end of bed and climb into bed by the dressing table.

I am not frightened but somewhat puzzled. I know that it is not my eyes because I would see pink everywhere. I hold the sheet up in front of me and that blacks everything out. When I put the sheet down, the bottom of the bed has disappeared into a wall of pink fog. I feel no emotion, I am in a state of suspended animation. The cloud comes slowly towards me so that it smothers me and I can't see anything but pink fog. Then it goes behind me and disappears through the wall. It goes through a part of the wall where there was a door many years ago. My sister, who is then about five years old, sleeps on the other side of the wall and as it goes into her room she cries out in her sleep. This brings me back into the real world and I am frightened. I try to shout but nothing comes out of my mouth. I roll out of bed and dive for the door and go into my parents' room which is on the landing above D. She says, 'Good God, you look as if you have seen a ghost!'. My father thinks I have been dreaming but I repeat the events to him. My mother suggests that I should go back to bed but not put the light out. I reply that nothing in earth would persuade me to put the light out. The next morning, my grandmother remarks, 'It's no wonder our electricity bills keep going up, your son has been at it again, last night he went to sleep over his books and left the light on!'.

A week later I went into hospital for what was expected to be a run-of-the-mill operation but which resulted in a long stay in the deep ray ward of the Queen Elizabeth with observation for the next thirteen years. Whether there is a coincidence or not I don't know, but, if you remember, the first appearance as such was a very short time before my grandmother died.

Ghosts ten a penny

Gemma Taylor* says that most hospitals have a number of ghost stories in circulation. They are ten a penny, especially on the geriatric wards. The night staff huddle round and out comes a ghost story or two. Here are two strange experiences which have come her way.

I am able to report these incidents with a clear conscience because all the hospital blocks referred to have now been demolished. In the first story I was the patient and in the second I was an auxiliary nurse.

When I was married in the 1950's I moved to Evesham and I was very unhappy. I didn't have any friends and I didn't know the area. A year later I was in the maternity hospital, then in Briars Close, giving birth to my first baby. There was only one midwife and one

The Leicester tower, built to commemorate the battle of Evesham

auxiliary on duty and they were very busy. I was in labour from the Monday night to midday Wednesday, I wasn't given anything to eat on the Tuesday and I was supposed to be having gas and air but it was discovered later that the machine hadn't been connected.

When the midwife and the auxiliary came in at twenty past one on the Wednesday afternoon I felt all but dead. They turned me onto my side and I had the strange feeling that a pair of eyes were boring into my back. I turned to look and I saw that the door was three parts covered by a screen and next to the screen was this figure, which I took to be a theatre nurse in a gown and mask, staring at me. The midwife kept trying to push me back and I kept turning to look at this figure. I felt as if I was floating and I distinctly heard the midwife say, 'We're going to lose her'. She gave me a slap which caught me on my neck and really hurt. At that moment my son was born. I looked for the figure, expecting her to be standing by the bed and I said to the midwife and the auxiliary, 'Where's she gone?' 'Who?' they asked. 'The nurse in the gown and mask?' They looked at each other and said, 'Oh my God!'.

I heard later that this apparition had been seen many times and it always visited those who were dying. It scared the living daylights out of me. The next day, I started shaking from the knees upwards.

Another strange experience occurred when I was an auxiliary nurse at Avonside Hospital during the 1960's. There were three of us on night duty on the geriatric ward, Mac (the staff nurse) and two auxiliaries, Lynne and myself. Even as we went on our way to the ward, before we had heard the reports, I said to Lynne, 'I don't think we're going to get a quiet night' and she said, 'I think you're going to be right'. And so it proved to be. Normally our aim was to get everyone tucked up by ten thirty but they all seemed to have picked up something and it was, 'Nurse, can I have a sandwich?', 'Nurse, come and talk to me' and so on. There was one patient who was making such a noise she kept all the others awake and at two in the morning it was decided to give her a dose of largactol.

Our shift was from eight pm until eight am and we were supposed to have an hour off for dinner but everyone wasn't quiet until three-thirty and we had to start again at four am. Mac said that it was ridiculous, we couldn't do another six hour stint on top of the last. She said we were to put our feet up for half an hour so we went into her tiny little office

and took a chair each. Lynne was next to me and I was opposite the door with my feet on a chair and my cloak over my legs. Mac said, 'I'm going to put the lights out for half-an-hour but for God's sake, don't go to sleep'. She turned the light off and about two minutes later we heard the scraping of slippers going past the door. We all jumped up. Mac said, 'Oh my God, there's a patient out of bed!'. I rushed out of the door and was hit by the cold, it was like going through a sheet of ice. The others followed me and there were the three of us shivering and covered with goose pimples.

Mac said to me, You check the patients in the small ward and I'll check the large ward with Lynne. We put the lights on dim and made sure that there was a head on each pillow. Every patient was in bed.

Afterwards we told other nurses and they said, 'Haven't you heard about the old lady? You have just had the same experience as we did.' Periodically an old lady used to walk along the corridor and stand by the office door. Many of the staff had heard it.

A message from Great Uncle Billy

This curious story is from a local schoolteacher, now retired.

My mother had to go into hospital for a cataract operation. Now, my mother has hospital phobia and the only way they got her in there was the specialist saying ' We will have you in tomorrow!'

At that time I was living and teaching in Evesham. That particular morning I was going to a service at the Methodist Chapel, but on the way I had to call in at the school to look after the animals in the natural history department. As I turned up at the school a voice said to me, 'You will get a message to your mother, won't you? You must tell your mother that her eyes will be alright'. While I went round everything in the laboratory, this voice continued to persist and by now I recognised it as coming from my great uncle Billy. I got to chapel and sat in the pew with the voice still nagging me. I said, 'Look, I can't get up in the middle of the sermon!'.

I can't say whether I spoke out loud or the conversation took place in my head.

When I got home my wife said to me, 'Your dinner's ready!' but I told her that I must first go down to the telephone box (there wasn't a 'phone in the house). I telephoned my father and confirmed that he was going to see my mother that afternoon. Then I added, 'Will you give her a message from Billy?'. Father replied, 'Oh, I didn't know Billy was so concerned, that is very nice of him' to which I replied, 'No, not Billy your friend, mother's uncle Billy!' and I repeated the message. Somewhere in my head someone seemed to put a telephone down.

When my father reached the hospital he found mother in a right old state. Something had happened with the drops, her eyes had haemorrhaged and she was convinced that she was going to lose her sight. My father was able to give her the message and reassure her.

Oh, I forgot to mention, uncle Billy had died nine months previously.

Celebrities at Evesham

During the nineteenth century, Evesham was considered to be a very desirable residential area. The family of the exiled French Emperor, then titled the Duc d'Orleans, came to live at Wood Norton in 1872, in the very grand house which is now the BBC training centre. Earlier in the century another international celebrity came to live in the town. The story of how his existence came to the notice of present-day inhabitants is a curious one, told here by Will Dallimore:'

> A few years ago we did some decorating for Liz Finney, a new customer of ours, who had recently moved into a house in Elm Road, Evesham. During our time there Liz told us that she was studying the piano, and practised regularly in the evenings. As it was summer at the time she played with the window open. It was whilst she was playing one evening that she heard a rustling sound from outside. It appeared to be coming from just beyond her garden fence. She turned round and looked out of the window but saw no-one, although she felt the presence of someone.
>
> Recently we returned to do some more decorating for Mrs Finney, and discovered that she still gets her 'visitor' albeit a presence, when she is practising the piano. We asked if it happened every time she played. She said she'd notice it was usually when she was practising from her book of piano studies *Gradus ad Parnassum* by Muzio Clementi.
>
> The name Muzio Clementi rang a bell, so we looked him up in a musical dictionary. Italian composer and piano virtuoso, born Rome 1752, died Evesham, Worcester, 1832. With further research we found that during his time at Evesham he lived at The Elm, a house, believe it or not, whose garden would have then run down to the far side of Liz Finney's fence.

Muzio Clementi was an infant prodigy and an accomplished organist by the age of nine. He was discovered by an English MP and brought to this country in 1770 when he gave concerts in London. In 1777 he conducted at the Italian Opera. He and Mozart were summoned to the court of Emperor Joseph II in Vienna to play competitively; the result was announced a draw. Clementi laid the foundation of modern pianoforte playing and, as illustrated by this story, his collection of studies, *Gradus ad Parnassum*, is still used.

Kidderminster. Hardly recognisable now, this is one of the roads leading up to the church in about 1939, before the construction of the ring road.

KIDDERMINSTER

As you pass the exit to Stourbridge on the ring road, driving towards the Bewdley exit, you pass very near to the spot where Henry III was nearly murdered in the thirteenth century. He was staying with John Biset, Lord of the Manor of Wolverhampton in his residential hall which was somewhere around (what is now) Dudley Street and Orchard Street, and near to the church. A relative of John's was also staying there, Margaret, and she was saying her prayers at midnight when she heard a slight noise and realised that an assassin was on his way to murder the king. She managed to raise the alarm and the king's life was saved. Part of the hall, including the kitchens, was later converted into a Brussels carpet factory which still existed in the nineteenth century.

Kidderminster was once the carpet manufacturing centre of the world. It lies on the river Stour, the waters of which contained Fuller's earth and iron, said to produce long-lasting dyes. The manufacture of cloths and carpets in Kidderminster goes back hundreds of years. By the time that Edward III spent three days at Kidderminster in 1332, so many townsmen were making and dyeing broad and narrow cloths that the trade had to be strictly regulated.

Early in the eighteenth century the cloth trade fell into decay, and was replaced by fancy materials, silks and woollens. One of Kidderminster's carpet manufacturers, John Broome, was concerned about the state of the industry so he travelled around Belgium and the Netherlands learning the latest techniques. He returned to England with a new type of loom from Brussels. The story goes that he tried to keep his loom secret and worked in a secluded garret in the Park Butts area, but a rival manufacturer climbed up a ladder at night and watched him working. The fact is that, by 1800, there were over a thousand looms of that type in Kidderminster and trade revived.

Apparitions in the factory

Alan Lauder, manager of the Kidderminster ghost walks, says that many old carpet factories still survive and some are haunted.

I used to work at Carpets of Kidderminster so I know that it had a ghost. The girls who were threading the looms have often sensed a presence, they felt that someone was looking over their shoulder but when they turned round, no-one was there. Sometimes a few of the employees would have to work all through the night to meet some deadline or other and they would often complain of strange experiences. Eric, the Works Manager, was working alone in the factory one night. To save electricity, the whole factory was in darkness except for the small area where he worked. About three o'clock in the morning he decided to make himself a cup of tea. He put the loom down, put the kettle on and, while he was waiting for the kettle to boil, he lit a cigarette. Suddenly, above his head, came the heavy, measured tread of footsteps. The roof was a typical factory roof made from glass and various other flimsy materials and it came to a sharp peak. No way could anyone be walking across it. Yet the footsteps began in one corner of the room and continued across until they reached the other corner of the room. He was so terrified that he refused to work alone overnight in the factory again.

The white witch of Worcester Street

Kidderminster was not only well-known for its carpets. People for miles around came to consult Becky Swan, said to be a white witch. She was born in 1771 and lived in the Worcester Street/Comberton Hill area together with a large number of dogs and cats. Becky had extraordinary healing powers and was probably a herbalist. When she was prosecuted for theft, she told the magistrate that he would die before she came out of jail. Her prophecy came true and her reputation was established.

There is a strange legend telling of her demise. In November 1850, an enormous black cat appeared in the village and stalked towards Becky's front door. Becky turned pale when she saw it but allowed it into the house. The cat was seen occasionally around the cottage over the next three day, but on the fourth day, the cat was not seen, neither was Becky. The doors remained locked and no smoke appeared from the chimney. Eventually neighbours broke down the door and went inside just in time to see the cat disappear up the chimney. Of Becky, there was no sign, but there was a mysterious heap of ashes in the middle of the floor.

An arresting story

Three of the roads leading to the present police station have the name Broomfield. This is because the police station was built on the site of Broomfield Hall. The Hall first appears in records in 1840, when it was a girl's boarding school under the supervision of Miss E Burgess.

Mr R G Emms joined the police force in 1960, when he was nineteen. It was his first time away from home and his first position was in Kidderminster. He continues:

> It was the same police station as it is now. I was told it was built on the site of Broomfield Hall and the occupiers met with a terrible end.
>
> In those days new recruits went straight to the police station and at Kidderminster, this story was always banded about. We would be told by the older men about the little grey lady who walked the police station. If I asked a question such as, 'Where does she walk?' they would tell me that it was unlucky to say too much about it. When there were a lot of people there you didn't think twice about it but when you were on your own with nothing to do, you began to hear all kinds of strange creaks and groans - and footsteps. I never found out whether it was true or false or a bit of each.
>
> When I went back to Kidderminster about ten years later as an inspector nobody ever talked about it. The old ones who were there at the time have passed away.

The question is, is the story true and what possible terrible end could occur in a school? In 1868 many of the pupils and staff of the Kidderminster schools went on an outing to the coast of North Wales. At Abergele, there was a terrible rail accident. Among those killed were the wife and daughter of the principal of the boys' school at Townsend House, Franche, and the two daughters of Mr Simcox Lea of Astley Hall. Perhaps Mr Lea's daughters attended the Broomfield school. The fact that the school came under new management that same year seems to confirm that it suffered heavily in the disaster.

The new principals, Miss Ridley and her cousin, Caroline Bennet, only remained at Broomfield Hall for a few months before they moved to the Girls' High School. Why did they move so suddenly? Did they, as well as the staff at the police station, see a little grey lady - perhaps one of the teaching staff - returning from the other world to continue her lessons?

The Workhouse

The first workhouse in Kidderminster was built in about 1783, halfway along Vicar Street on the same side as the Town Hall. It housed mostly orphans and the very elderly. Thirty years later a new one was built in the Oxford Street/Worcester Cross area. As the population expanded, a still larger one became necessary which was erected in what is now Broad Street. It was extended and developed to become the Union Workhouse of 1837/8 and then taken over to become the Kidderminster General Hospital in Bewdley Road. The corner building is the original workhouse. Where E block now stands, opposite St John's Church, was once a row of cottages. In one of these cottages lived Mrs P and her daughter.

My mum was a sister in Casualty and well-known to the hospital employees. Our family was friendly with a young hospital worker by the name of John who lived over the road. He came and knocked on my door one morning and he - well - looked as if he had seen a ghost. He was quite white. He said that he had been going along the walkway from the mortuary to Quales carpet factory on his bike and he had seen what he thought was a hospital porter in a grey cow gown. Then he realised that whatever-it-was was walking with his knees on the ground. The apparition had disappeared through an old doorway that once led into the old workhouse.

Old Mrs Whatmore was buried in St John's churchyard in the 1800's and someone else that day was scattering ashes over Mrs Whatmore's grave. Evidently she didn't like sharing her grave with somebody else. She came back to say, 'Hey, this is my bit'. He had to have five cigarettes and two whiskies before he felt better.

The grey lady of Mill Street

Susan has been nursing for well over twenty years. For three years she worked at the old Mill Street Hospital, which has now been converted into apartments, and more recently, for ten years she worked at Kidderminster General in Bewdley Road, now known as the Kidderminster Healthcare NHS Trust.

I was only eighteen when I went to Mill Street as a probationary nurse. The place was like a rabbit warren, very eerie, dark with half lights. The older nurses used to wind you up. They would say, 'You know this place is haunted, don't you?'. They told us about a grey lady seen coming down the stairs. Some of the nurses used to say, 'I've seen her' and they were quite sensible people, not the type to pull your leg. There was a chapel on the second floor and it was said that if the door opened all by itself there was going to be a death. You were alright until we went on night duty and then, when you were sitting all alone, you would be terrified.

When I worked in Kidderminster General in Bewdley road, I was in the old ITU unit, where the pharmacy is now, it was the old C block. There was one particular side ward where nothing would go right. Crucial items used to go missing and drips used to get turned on or altered when nobody was around. It didn't happen anywhere else, only in that side ward. Once, in the early hours of the morning, the monitor switched itself on. It was like those that you see on the telly, going bleep, bleep, bleep, and it was going crazy. No-one was in there except for the patient and he was fast asleep. The atmosphere suddenly went icy cold and it felt very oppressive, not nice at all. We turned the heating up full blast but it didn't seem to make any difference. It was really scarey.

We had got a night sister at that time who was a bit of a healer so we rang her up and explained what had happened. She came and sat in that side ward. I don't know what she did, she had her hands together, and in a few minutes the atmosphere lifted. Then it got really warm because, of course, we had the heating on full blast.

We asked her what had happened, and she reminded us that a couple of weeks before we had had a patient who had tried to commit suicide by walking under a bus. She had died later in that ward. This sister said that she needed help to get over to the other side - well, that's what she said. Anyway, it worked. The patient slept through all this commotion.

Nothing else has happened since we moved into our new unit.

Dastardly deeds at the Town Hall
by Alan Lauder, manager of the Kidderminster ghost walks

On the opening night of our first ghost walk Val related this story to the crowd. She belongs to an old Kidderminster family, her husband's grandfather was postmaster of Kidderminster and she heard the story from one of her elderly aunts.

Where you are now standing, in front of the Town Hall, there once stood a public house of some ill-repute. The Fleece was on this site from the 17th century and was quite notorious for its shifty dealings in the town. There had been a building on the site from early times and it is rumoured that there is beneath the current building, Kidderminster Town Hall, the remains of a Tudor crypt. The Fleece pub was, it is said, the spit and sawdust sort that Charles Dickens made famous in his novel *Oliver Twist* and, like that novel, had its own brand of villains. Thieves and ladies of the night frequented its smoky rooms and gin-ridden mothers set on their own ruinous path were to be seen on the dirty steps leading to its front door. It was one of the many prostitutes who used the pub to pick up her clients who was to bring this dim corner of Victorian Kidderminster to the notice of the more respectable townsfolk in a violent and bloody way. After taking her third client of the night and relieving him of both his lust and his wallet she had gone back into the smoky interior of the Fleece and was looking at the contents of her ill-gotten gains, when the door burst open and the owner of the wallet she had stolen burst in through the door. Needless to say the man was not too pleased at being robbed and he lunged at the woman in an attempt to get back his rightful property. Grabbing her by the arm he threatened to drag her to the police station. She put up a very spirited fight and her loud screaming aroused from his drunken slumber her husband who relied upon her earnings for his alcohol. He drew his knife and stabbed at the man who was still wrestling with the woman and wallet, unfortunately, he was so drunk that his aim was not true and the woman fell to the floor, mortally wounded. The police were sent for and arrived shortly after to find the woman lying dead upon he floor and her husband clutching his throat with blood pouring from between his fingers. He had slashed his own throat and he died shortly afterwards.

Of the man there was no sign and no-one in the pub could begin to describe him other that he was well-dressed and not very tall. The wallet lay on the floor, its contents gave no clue to the man's identity as all it contained was a lock of blond hair tied with a ribbon.

Dastardly deeds were committed on the site of Kidderminster town hall

Despite having two new corpses the police did not feel it was necessary to find the man. The wallet was removed to the police station and the case was closed before it really began, shortly afterwards the pub was demolished to make way for the new town hall building.

There have been, over the years, many reports of the shadowy figure of a man, quite small in stature, being seen, late at night, around the town hall buildings. He is on his knees, patting the ground, he appears to be searching for something.

The long wait

Kidderminster has been described as a town which is always undergoing alterations but never seems to improve. A minor change which is regretted by many of the old townsfolk is the closure of the local chemist, Trevethick's, which was in the Bull Ring opposite the General Post Office. Mrs V bought a bench from the shop when it closed down.

A little old lady lives in my kitchen. I have seen her at various times, particularly when going into the laundry room. I mostly notice her as I'm going past. The cats don't seem to bother about her but next door's dog will occasionally bristle. I don't know who she is. She just sits on the bench. We bought the bench when we first moved here and at that time she came more regularly than she does now. Patients used to sit on the bench and wait for their prescriptions. I can't see her distinctly, she's more of a grey misty shape than anything, but I can see that she's a pleasant old soul, quite rotund, and she wears a longish dress. It seems as if she is looking at us as if we are on television. She just sits there, almost as if she's taking in what is going on, as though she was checking us out, to see what we were like. She seems to have accepted us now.

Here are two short anecdotes, both have a similar theme.

A visit from grandpa.

When my son was four he came belting into our bedroom at seven o'clock in the morning to tell us that a ghost had been to see him. Within ten minutes my husband's mother was on the telephone to say that his grandfather had died in Offmoore Nursing Home.

A visit from a dear friend

Just before Christmas, this year, I had a very dear friend, a man, who was very ill. I was just going out into the garden at ten to eight in the morning when I saw a black cloud behind me and I had the impression that it was a man. I didn't actually see a man, I just had the feeling that it was a man. When his relatives phoned me to tell me that he had passed away I said that I knew what time he had died, it was ten to eight, and I was right.

Mother comes home

About a week ago a friend of mine was redecorating the lounge and suddenly, a bag full of my mum's odds and ends fell down. It had been set very firmly on the chair next to her and there was no reason why it should have fallen down. My friend was using two paintbrushes, one large and one smaller. While she was using the large one she put the smaller one at her feet on a piece of newspaper. When she went to get it the brush had gone. She said, 'Where is it? You're messing me around here, aren't you?'. Eventually we found it on the other side of the room with no newspaper underneath. Now who would put a paintbrush full of paint straight on to the carpet? Another strange fact was that it hadn't left any marks on the carpet. I told her that it wasn't me but probably my mum who was messing her about.

She didn't like that, but it's true. I lost my mother about six years ago but I can still sense that she is around. She likes to make her existence known and I would say that, starting from the evening of the funeral, something happens about once every two months.

There was one night when I couldn't sleep. I lay on the settee with my eyes closed, but I know that I wasn't asleep. Suddenly, I felt something brush against my cheeks. I quickly opened my eyes but nothing was there.

At another time there was a scroll pinned up in the kitchen door. It was a wooden one and it flew six or seven feet across the room in front of me, landing about two feet away. I picked it up. I also hear her footsteps on the landing - I sense her existence most acutely in her bedroom. And when I get talking about my mum a book or something falls off the mantelpiece. Weird little things happen.

There was a time that I happened to be looking in the mirror and when I turned, it was as if someone was there. It was such a shock that my whole body shook. One evening, I was listening to music downstairs on the settee when I sensed that somebody was there in the corner and as I turned round I could see this mist. I know the difference between cigarette smoke and a mist, and anyway, I don't smoke. This mist was very fine, you could see through it, and although it had no shape it was about body height. It was there for a minute before it faded.

Most things happen in the evening when I am on my own. I spend a lot of time on my own. It's as if she is saying, 'Everything is going to be OK'. She's not only on the outside, but also on the inside of me. Often I say things and I think, 'That's not me talking, it's my mum'.

It doesn't frighten me, I always talk to her. I feel that she is watching over me.

The British Camp in the Malvern Hills

THE MALVERNS

n the southern end of the hills are two great peaks, the Worcestershire Beacon and the Herefordshire Beacon. Both are nearly 1,400 feet high. The Herefordshire Beacon is often referred to as 'the British Camp'. It was here, about 1,900 years ago, that over a thousand ancient Britons gave their lives in a last desperate stand against the Romans.

The Herefordshire Beacon and the adjacent Midsummer Hill were once an enormous Iron Age fortress, its slopes covered with stone walls and ramparts. It must have seemed impregnable. The lower rampart had a circumference of two miles and the whole fort covered an area of about forty-five acres, large enough to hold a small army. The hill was used in prehistoric times, perhaps as a religious centre, but under the threat of Roman invasion it was strengthened and developed by the Ancient Britain's. Their hero was Caracatus (or Caractacus) and legend sugests that it was here that Caracatus fought his final battle.

Whoever fortified the camp expected the Romans to attack from the east and on that side, the works are the strongest. However, they attacked from the West, creeping along the Wye valley and the thick woodland covering the hills. They went straight for the centre of a great Western rampart. Being convex it was unprotected but its slopes were the steepest and the most difficult. After breaching the outer wall the Romans advanced, shields locked, swords hacking and stabbing. The Britons had neither breast plates nor helmets to save them from the Roman swords. The Romans had the reputation of slaughtering their enemies without mercy. The Herefordshire Beacon stands as a memorial to the thousand or more who died defending our shores from invaders.

Caracatus managed to escape and fled into Yorkshire to hide at his stepmother's, Queen of the Brigantes. Unfortunately, his stepmother was anxious to placate the Romans, so she put him chains and handed him over to the Romans. Their General sent Caracatus and his family to Rome. When he was brought before the Roman emperor, Caracatus said, 'How is it that you, who dwell in such grand palaces, envy us poor Britons our thatched cottages?'. The emperor decreed that his chains should be removed and Caracatus is thought to have settled in Rome.

At the other end of the hills, in the centre of Great Malvern, is the church of Malvern Priory. Ancient documents tell of the founding of the Priory in 1085, by a hermit named Alwy who lived with a single male companion in 'the vast wilderness which is called Malvern'. One monk after another came to join him until they numbered about 300. Nothing is left of the Priory except for a wall and a gateway at the front of the present church. This church originally belonged to the Priory and the townsfolk had a modest little church which fitted into the north west corner of the present churchyard. When the townsfolk saw this beautiful church, with its fascinating misericords, beautiful stained glass windows, they were consumed with envy and were determined to acquire it for themselves. Their opportunity came when Henry VIII dissolved many monasteries for they were able to buy it for £20.

Unfortunately, there was some confusion about who should supervise the Priory, which lead to one of the greatest ecclesiastical disputes on record. The Bishop of Worcester considered that the Priory was under his supervision whereas Alwy had put it under the care of Westminster Abbey 'for the time being'. In 1282 it came to the notice of the Bishop of Worcester that the prior, William de Ledbury, was keeping twenty-two women at various houses and farms connected with the Priory. The Bishop of Worcester deposed him and excommunicated any monk who supported William. Despite being excommunicated, the monks elected another prior, and sent him to Westminster to be blessed. The Abbot of Westminster clapped the new prior into prison 'loaded with fetters', together with all his followers. The Bishop of Worcester appealed to the king and the pope and pronounced excommunication after excommunication but to no avail. Eventually, William de Ledbury was reinstated, the new prior and his followers were released from prison, the excommunications were all withdrawn and the Bishop of Worcester was given a piece of land for his pains.

With such a large and colourful monastery based here, it comes as no surprise to find the townsfolk bumping into the odd ghostly monk.

Christmas spirit
Madresfield

Madresfield is a tiny village about half a mile from Great Malvern. Will Mound says that he has told many people about this incident:

> I didn't believe in ghosts until I actually saw one. It was about thirty years ago but I can still see it clearly in my mind.
>
> I used to cycle to and from work along Rectory Lane in Madresfield village. About two days before Christmas I saw, on the bank, in the gardens of the Old Rectory, a holly bush loaded with berries. I thought, 'On the way home, I will take a sprig'. It was six o'clock when I left work. I stopped in Rectory Lane, there was no mist and the night was perfectly clear. It was a full moon, and as you   know, the moon destroys colour so that the berries and the leaves both looked   the same colour and it was difficult to choose a good branch. I   looked down the lane and about thirty yards away, in the   direction from which I had come, was a tall,   dark silhouette of a monk. Although, as I   have said, colour was destroyed by the full moon,   the colour of his robe stood out as being a browney grey. He had a tall, pointed hat and he made no noise. His robes stopped a few inches above the ground. It was very vivid. I stood there with my bicycle, ready to jump on it. He advanced, walking towards me. I hadn't passed him as I cycled that way and there was no gate through which he could have appeared. I couldn't make out any details, he was just a dark silhouette.
>
> It scared me to bits. I jumped on my bike and pedalled home as fast as I could go. I lived about half a mile away. When I got home I slammed the door. My wife said, 'What's the matter with you, you're as white as a sheet, you look as if you have seen a ghost' and I replied, 'That's just it, you have said it'.
>
> I have been down the road many times since but I've never seen him again. About 300 or 400 yards away is the main road from Newland to Worcester and my daughter says that whenever she drives that way, she always feels as if someone is on the back seat.

The shopping trolley apparition
A449

Will's daughter is not the only one to have had a strange experience on that stretch of road, as Lynne Smith testifies:

> It was about eight o'clock one Friday night in October or November in, I think, 1987, that my husband and I were on our way to a Rotary Club dinner and dance at Malvern. We were on the A449 at Newland, when suddenly an elderly lady stepped out into the road with her shopping trolley and my husband had to swerve violently to avoid her. I can see

her in my mind's eye now. She was grey-haired and quite plump and she was wearing a red coat. She was right in front of us and she turned and looked full into the headlights. She was going from some cottages across to the pub.

I said to my husband, 'Have you caught her?'. If we had not hit her the car behind must have done so. He stopped the car, turned round and went back. We fully expected to see a crowd round a body on the floor, but there was nothing - no body, no crowd, no ambulance, nothing.

When we arrived at the dinner we were both shaking. It had been very clear and we hadn't been drinking or anything like that.

It has only recently occurred to me that what we saw was a ghost. I said to my husband, 'That was a ghost we saw that night, you know'. He said, 'Oh, I know that but I didn't say anything because I didn't want to frighten you'.

Uncle pays a visit
Malvern Link

Before arriving at the centre of Malvern town on the A449, just below the North Hill, there are a few shops, some nice detached houses and a roadway across a common. This is Malvern Link. Mrs Griffiths, who tells the next story, is a very sensible, down-to-earth person, now married to a retired farmer in Leominster.

I moved to Summerfield Road in Malvern Link in the late 1970's. I was working in my kitchen one morning when I happened to look out of the window and saw a strange man in my garden. He didn't look like an itinerant, he was very smartly dressed in a grey suit. He was slim, fairly elderly - I would say in his sixties - and very erect. There he was, facing the door of my shed not far from my garden gate.

I rushed out of the kitchen to see what he wanted. The door of the kitchen was right by the window so it only took a second or two and when I got outside, he was nowhere to be seen. I had a good look round and I could see for some way - we backed on to allotments - and there was nowhere he could have gone.

A week or two later I went to get my shopping from the Co-op in Malvern Link. I was chatting to the girl at the cash desk and she asked me where I had moved to. When I told her, she said, 'That was my uncle's house'. I said, 'We bought it from the so-and-so's' (I forget the name). She replied, 'He lived there before they did'. I asked her what he looked like and she described the man I had seen in the garden. He had died a year or two beforehand.

A slip in time
Blackmore Park Industrial Estate

The pure Malvern air would make it an ideal location for a hospital. During the last war, the Americans had the reputation of having the biggest and the best of everything, and it is therefore quite logical that they should have a Military Airforce hospital here.

During the late 1980s I was working at the Blackmore Park Industrial Estate in Malvern with a company that builds trailers. These individual industrial units were originally the various sections of a hospital. The hospital had first been a military one with Nissan huts but then the Americans took it over and turned it into a splendid American Airforce hospital. It was one of the biggest in the country.

Quite a few people have funny tales to tell about those industrial units. I'm a welder; you have a mask down over your face and anything behind you is often reflected into the mask at the front. Quite frequently, I would think that there was someone behind but when I turned round, nobody would be there, when I could have sworn that I saw the reflection of somebody. However, I thought nothing of it. Quite a few times - it happened to other workers as well as me - you would put a tool down and suddenly it would be somewhere else. One thing I remember was that I bought a fluorescent pink tape measure so that I could spot it easily in all the clutter on my bench. I would put it down, then go to grab it and it would be gone. It would be over the other side of the workshop or somewhere quite impossible where I had not been. It would just move, often when nobody else was there. We mentioned this to the person that we worked for but he was the type who did not believe in anything strange going on. He was very sceptical.

I was often the only one there and it was one evening when I was on my own that something happened which really put the wind up me. I had been working over and it was about seven o'clock on a bright summer evening. The sun was just touching the tops of the Malvern Hills but it had not gone down. I was preparing to leave the building so I checked the windows to make sure they were all closed, then I went outside, closed the main doors (not locking them as I was expecting my boss to return any minute) and went to get into my car. The car parking area is right in front of the industrial unit and my car was parked in front of the main doors but slightly to the left so that the bonnet was almost touching the first window. As I opened my door I happened to glance up at this window and noticed that it was freshly-painted and open. I thought, 'Oh, I've left that window open' and I went back into the building to close it. To my surprise, I found that it was closed. Then I realised that the present window was rusty, cracked and dirty and I had seen a nice new window with smart brickwork all round it. Later, I remembered that it could not possibly have been open because a few months earlier I had been asked to weld it closed for security reasons. The quarter light at the top of each side could open but not the main window.

I thought, 'Am I seeing things?'. I was so unnerved that, although I'm not a drinker, I had a quick drink on the way home. Even now, I feel queer thinking about it.

The shadow of death

Was Anne Toombs'* mother thinking of her just before she passed away and did Anne pick this up by some kind of telepathy?

> My mother was very, very ill in a nursing home in Malvern. I stayed with her all day, but in the evening she was on pethadine and unconscious. The sister in charge said that she would prefer it if I left in the evening and she promised to ring at six the next morning or if she needed me in the night.
>
> A friend of mine who lived nearby had invited me to stay with her, which I did, parking my car so that it was facing the home so that I could rush there if anything happened. I went to bed and was off to sleep in a few minutes. I had nothing on my conscience, I had done everything that I could.
>
> It was about two-ish when I woke up as lively as a cricket. I became conscious of the distinct noise of heavy breathing, of the cheyne-stoke type. It came from a certain area of the room; from the top left corner of the room near the window. I was not at all afraid and felt perfectly relaxed. I remember listening to it for several minutes and looking at my watch. I am certain that I wasn't dreaming.
>
> I was awoken by the phone; it was matron. I said, 'It's alright Matron, I know that mother passed away'. Matron said, 'How do you know?'
>
> The strange thing was that, although I was the only child, mother and I were not all that close.

The Redan Bend

If you drive from Worcester to Malvern along the A449, you will find that at the foot of the North Hill a road branches off on the right, known as the North Malvern Road. It runs along the side of the North Hill, past a clock tower and a quarry, then there's a nasty bend. This is the Redan Bend. There was once a public house here, huge and barracks-like, called the Redan. It was built sometime during the 1860's and derived its name from a stronghold in Sebastopol, Russia. Perhaps the original builder made his money fighting in the Crimean War of 1854-55, when the siege of Sebastopol was one of the principal incidents.

Eventually the owner went bankrupt. Fortunately the public house had been built like a fortress and he was able to barricade himself in during the day so that the bailiffs were unable to gain access. He only emerged late at night and eventually died in the building. Later occupiers declared that the building was haunted. Dark shadows were seen flitting from room to room and strange noises could be heard throughout the night. The pub was demolished in 1978.

PERSHORE AND WICK

ershore Abbey is one of the Midland's great treasures, very old and very beautiful. It is thought to have been founded as long ago as 689 by King Oswald, then destroyed in 976 and rebuilt about a thousand years ago. Despite a fire in 1288, much of the building dates back to the 1100's.

Today, the main entrance to the abbey park is through a pair of wrought iron gates with a coat of arms on each side. Five hundred years ago, at this point, you would have been walking into the abbey itself for this is where the original building ended. When Henry VIII ordered the huge abbey complex to be pulled down, the people of Pershore paid £400 to save just the eastern half of the abbey church, the chancel. There were other buildings such as the Refectory and the Cloisters stretching right across the present grassy area.

The monks here were the black-robed Benedictines, following the strict rules of Saint Benedict. Their motto was *laborare est orare*, to work is to pray. Their day was divided into three parts, the first in prayer, the second in work in the cloister (writing and translating) and the third was more on the manual side, woodworking, or at the forge or in the fields. The first service of the day was at two in the morning! The Benedictines founded schools (most of the older universities grew out of Benedictine schools), drained swamps and brought land under cultivation.

Fred and the fire station

Their work would have frequently taken them down to the river. About a quarter of a mile to the south east from the abbey, the River Avon runs alongside the A44. To reach this point the monks would probably have walked along (what is now) part of Defford Road and past the Fire Station. Some of the Fire Officers suspect that a monk still walks that way, as described by one of the firemen.

I have been a fireman here for ten years or so; I was told about the ghost when I first came, I have heard him myself and I know that he still makes regular visits. Everyone affectionately calls him Fred.

The story goes that during the last war, the old building which is now the Fire Station was turned into an ATS drill hall, and the cellars were converted into a rifle range. These alterations evidently disturbed Fred who put in an appearance, with the result that one of the ATS girls thought she had shot somebody! There was quite a to-do.

I was down there late one evening with four other Fire Officers - this is going back about ten years - when a locate curate dropped in. We were all talking and joking and he said, 'For a bit of fun, let's hold a seance'. So we scribbled numbers and letters on bits of card and laid them out and sat round with a finger on the glass. Then the glass started wandering round, we were all accusing each other of pushing it. It started spelling out a lady's name, but for the life of me, I can't remember what the name was. The next thing was, at two minutes to twelve, the lights went out. I was over the desk and out the door and the two girls ran out. I don't know what was going on. There was no-one about who could have switched the lights off. We assumed that Fred was getting annoyed with us because we were laughing and joking about him.

One lad, Tony, was on watch duty and he had a fire shout at a quarter to twelve. He was writing up his log afterwards and something frightened him so much that he stopped writing and ran away. You can still see in one of the books where his writing suddenly stops in the middle of a sentence.

Fred still pays us a visit nearly every week. You can guarantee that round about midnight the Appliance Room (the old cellar) will go quite cold and no manner of heating will get it warm.

Then suddenly, you can hear a man's footsteps walking at a normal, leisurely pace. They come in through the front doors, walk straight through all the vehicles and go out of the door which leads into the funeral parlour. It does the same route every time. People have suggested that it might be something to do with the Abbey. When Pershore Abbey was at its height there was an old monastery to the south of the church, and historians say that a pathway once went this way from the monastery down to the river.

The ghost is very well known. We used to have a club down there when a lot of people heard the footsteps. The ambulance people have also heard them and at one time, no-one from the ambulance station would stay overnight, although Fred doesn't hurt anybody.

Haunted Wick

The A44 runs from Pershore Abbey to Evesham Abbey. As the houses of Pershore peter out, so the picturesque buildings of Wick begin, hidden away on the northern side of the road.

At the rear of the Pershore Abbey are two memorials to the Hazlewood family. They were great land-owners between 1520 and 1745 and although they originally came from Yorkshire and Northamptonshire they chose the lovely village of Wick in which to settle and were Lords of the Manor.

The history of Wick is so incredible that if someone were to present it as a novel no-one would believe it. Two of its owners were beheaded and the Manor House was lost in a game of cards. It has belonged to both Henry VIII's fifth wife and to Elizabeth I.

In 1066 Wick was held by Pershore Abbey, later by the Abbey of Westminster. At the dissolution it went to Henry VIII who gave it to Catherine Parr. She sold it to Sir Anthony Babington who lived in it for five years before he went to the tower in the Babington plot. It then fell into the hands of Queen Elizabeth who gave it to Sir Walter Raleigh who also ended up in the Tower. Therefore two of the owners were beheaded within six years.

From there it went into the hands of the Hazlewood family whose tombs are in the back of Pershore Abbey. Charles Hudson, who now lives at the Manor House, has been told by his family that about 250 years ago there was a mega game of cards at the House which ended up with the Hazlewoods heavily in debt to the Hudsons. The Hudsons therefore came into ownership of the Manor House. In 1994, a couple of members of the Hazlewood family called there. The same story had circulated in their family. Mr Hudson said that he would show them round the house but he wasn't going to play another game of cards!

Charles Hudson's grandfather owned garments which he said belonged to Charles II. He said that Charles II stayed at Wick House during the civil war and left some of his garments there. They were sold in the 1940s/1950s.

The lovely half-timbered frontage of Wick Manor only dates back to the early 1920's. Part of the house was reconstructed as a kind of memorial to the heir of the household, Lieut Alban John Benedict Hudson MC. He fell in love and his parents thought he was too young to marry; they therefore decided, as he had joined up, to ask his commanding officer to post him elsewhere. He was killed at the battle of Messines on 7 June 1917. In the house is a chapel containing an alabaster effigy of the young man. His parents also built houses for disabled ex-servicemen in the village.

The Hudson family have lived in the area for so long it would be surprising if there were not an ancestor or two wandering around. Stan has lived in Wick for many years and says:

One of the Hudson family, Burnell, went into the priesthood and became a monk at Pershore. He died earlier this century when he was quite young. He was very eccentric, for example, he insisted on using the old road into Pershore instead of the new one, climbing over stiles and walking through hedges. The old road to Wick was changed in about the 1700 but you can still see where it used to be in the fields if you know where to look.

There have been two sightings of monks just where the old London road used to turn in front of Wick House. Both sightings were at seven am. The last one was by a very down-to-earth man who works in the offices of a local factory. He was walking his dog one January morning when a figure came by dressed in a monk's habit and making no sound. When he looked again there was nobody there. His wife phoned me that morn

Wick manor, built in 1923 round a Georgian core, is the home of the Hudson family

ing to see if I knew of any ghost stories about a monk. I remembered that I had heard that about twenty years ago, about the same time in the morning, when it was pitch dark, someone else had seen the ghost of a monk.

Traditionally, Wick is haunted by a lady in red. However, she seems to have changed her costume over the past decade or so and now puts in the occasional appearance wearing blue. Before Charles Hudson moved into Wick Manor one of the flats was rented by a Mr A O Jones and he saw the blue lady. He told the locals:

I know I'm a hard-headed businessman but I saw what I saw.

Charles Hudson also caught a glimpse of her.

As I was going out of the bathroom I looked into my sister's bedroom and I saw a woman standing by the window. I assumed it was my sister, partly because she had been wearing a dark blue pullover and trousers and this person was wearing dark clothing. I only gave her a casual glance and didn't really take it in, but I do remember that I could see the silhouette of a slim female wearing a garment down to the floor. I went downstairs into the kitchen and there was my sister. I said, 'Wasn't that you upstairs?' She said 'Don't be ridiculous, I'm down here, how could I be upstairs?'. My brother-in-law was in the kitchen with her and he said that she'd been there for some time.

The Dower House, the beautiful old Van Dyke Court, still stands at the western end of the village. The Lady of the Manor would have moved into this house on the death of her husband.

The Fraser family lived at Van Dyke Court for five years but although they heard about a lady in red, none of them saw her. Karsalie Fraser says:

My parents bought the house in 1955 and the family moved in during the autumn. We never experienced any ghostly happenings, perhaps because my father was a retired Church of England clergyman and my two sisters and I were all adult and working - ie no teenagers. After we had been living there for a year or so, a family of three maiden ladies and their bachelor brother (all now deceased) did ask me if we had seen the lady, and proceeded to tell us that she had been seen at various times before the war, I think by the lady who then lived at Van Dyke Court.

During the war the RAF had rented or requisitioned the house to accommodate thirty or forty WAAF, and the owners before us made no mention of ghostly apparitions (but if they wished to sell the house perhaps they would keep quiet about such happenings!).

In 1960 my parents decided to build a house in Drakes Broughton and Van Dyke Court was sold to Mr and Mrs Havard who wished to move out from Birmingham to live nearer their factory in Blackminster (Evesham).

Mrs Havard states that she, too, has never seen a lady in red, however ...

We came here in October 1961 and in the November we would wake up to hear a rat-tat-tat like cannon fire going on outside our bedroom. My husband would get up and go out on the landing to find that the noise seemed to be coming from the top of the stairs just in front of him. Once or twice I got out of bed to see what it was all about but I would generally get in the way - I would bump into him and he would think I was the ghost. This went on for a few nights on and off all through that winter. It couldn't have been banging pipes because we didn't have central heating in those days. We looked for all kinds of explanations but we didn't discover what it was.

Each morning I would go into my study (the room by the front door) to pull the curtains. Once or twice I went in and I felt as if someone had got up from the easy chair by the window and walked right past me. I thought, 'This is ridiculous' and I didn't say anything to my husband.

Not long after that I was in the kitchen and just about to begin washing up after

The Dower House, Van Dyke Court, at Wick

breakfast when I heard an orchestra playing *Swan Lake*. I thought my son or my daughter must have left the radio on upstairs. They left the house at 8.35 each morning when my husband took them to school and at that time, in those days, there used to be radio intermission when a piece of music was played for about five minutes. I assumed that this was what I was hearing. Just at that moment the plumber arrived to do some work. I said to him, 'I'll come upstairs with you as I think one of the children has left a radio on' but both radios were switched off. The only other radio was the one in the kitchen and I knew that wasn't on. About a week later, I went to lunch with some friends and I happened to mention the incident. One of them was very interested and he got in touch with the BBC and asked them what music they were playing on that day. I had a little card from the BBC and I can't remember what music it was but it wasn't Swan Lake. This was a bit intriguing.

Some mornings I would go to do the washing up and I would feel there was a shadow by the kitchen door. I would turn round to see who it was but there wouldn't be anybody there. Of course, I didn't mention it to anyone.

One night my husband and came home a bit earlier because we were going to the theatre in Birmingham. My husband went upstairs to the bathroom and as he was came out he looked into our bedroom and saw a woman in blue sitting at the dressing table in front of the mirror. Thinking it was me he said something, at which my daughter called out, 'If you're talking to mother she's not here'. He said that I was there and that he had just spoken to me. My daughter replied that I wasn't in the house and that I had just popped out to Pershore. He swears to this day that he definitely saw a woman in blue at my dressing table.

After this we got together and pooled our experiences but we never came up with anything specific.

A short while later we began to employ an odd-job man, and I said to him, 'While you are here, could you get up those four flagstones outside the garage?'. The drive was going to be tarmacked and I wanted it extended. These flags were old tomb stones that the Fraser's had brought with them and all that they had on them were the initials of the deceased person. He pulled them up and put them on the side of the garden. After that, this poor man had one piece of bad luck after another. He was seriously ill, then his wife was ill, then he had a motor bike accident.

A few weeks after the stones had been moved, a man came to do the tarmac and at the same time, we went on holiday. When we returned the stones had disappeared. The strange thing is that nothing out of the ordinary happened after that. Whatever it was seemed to have been tied up with the stones. I asked Mrs Fraser if she knew where they had come from.

Karsalie Fraser was able to give the full history of the stones.

My father's last parish before retiring was Hertingfordbury, on the outskirts of Hertford, with two other small hamlets. We moved into the Rectory with its very overgrown garden but gradually we were able to clear it out and convert it into a nice garden. When removing a large bank of brambles and rubble to site a second garage, our gardener came across a lot of (mostly broken) tombstones. My father enquired of his Churchwardens how the stones got there and was told that the previous, rather eccentric, incumbent had purloined a lot of tombstones from the churchyard a few years back, hoping that no-one would mind if he made a patio or something with them - but the parishioners did mind! However, it was decided to be impracticable to return them and so the Rector had buried them behind the drive hedge. We only stayed two years before my father decided to retire, and when doing various alterations to the house and garden at Van Dyke, my parents decided we might as well use the slabs.

The last word goes to Mrs Havard, who says that she hopes that whoever took the stones has brought upon himself all the bad luck suffered by the odd job man!

REDDITCH

edditch, like Evesham and Pershore, is an abbey town. It developed to cater for the needs of Bordesley Abbey, the Abbey came first and the town developed round it. In the early 1100's, Worcestershire had many ecclesiastical houses but they all belonged to the black-robed Benedictines. The eleven white-robed monks who arrived in Redditch round about 1140 established the first Cistercian abbey in Worcestershire. The Cistercian order was much more severe and strict than the Benedictine.

Bordesley Abbey flourished and eventually owned over twenty farms or granges in Worcestershire and Warwickshire. Its demise came in the middle of the fourteenth century with the Black Death or Bubonic plague, when at least a quarter of the population died. This, and poor harvests, meant that by 1381 only fourteen monks were left. The plague did not disappear altogether but recurred every ten or twenty years. The last severe national outbreak was in the year of the Fire of London, 1665.

Although the Black Death was the most severe, throughout the centuries Redditch people have had to contend with other epidemics. The word 'Cholera' would put fear into every mother's heart. In 1832 a national epidemic raged but there were 'few places in the kingdom was it more deadly than in Redditch'. There was such a terrible succession of deaths that some townsfolk left the area. Only six years later there was a terrible epidemic of Smallpox when some families lost several children. The licensee of the Horse and Jockey buried five children in three weeks, four children died from the Webb family and Henry Humphries lost three of his four children.

In addition, in the small town of Redditch at least one child per year died from each of the infectious diseases such as scarlet fever, measles, whooping cough and diptheria. In times of epidemics the death toll could be a score or more. Bronchitis, pneumonia and pulmonary tuberculosis also killed forty or more each year, many of them infants.

The Medical Officer of Health reported that the death toll was not that of a country town but equal to a crowded inner city. In 1875 twenty-three streets were without sewers and fifty-eight houses had no water supply. 458 houses had uncovered middens. People mostly obtained their water from pumps or wells and as many as 120 people could share one well.

Another reason for the high death rate was the terrible conditions in needle factories. Redditch was the needle-making capital of the world. It had once been a cottage industry but by the 1870's the industrial revolution had moved people into factories. People were working long hours in unhealthy environments. At a time when women were not expected to work, Redditch women did so and the Medical Officer of Health complained that many babies were put out to care, often to 'wet' nurses.

Tales my grandmother told me
Mount Pleasant

The first ghost story, by Ken Andrews, is set in this uncertain world of the 1800's. Behind the Quality Hotel in Mount Pleasant is Torrs Close and tucked away at the end is a splendid Victorian house, the Torrs.

My grandmother was born in 1850 and she told me this story:

Mrs Gibbons had a house on Mount Pleasant and she scraped and saved until, one by one, she managed to buy a house for each of her children, who were then teenagers. All the houses were at the top of Mount Pleasant, opposite the old Council House and by the Torrs. Then she died and an uncle came along and turned all these children out and put them into care. So she returned to each of these houses as a ghost, frightening out the occupants.

On one of these occasions, a neighbour arrived home to find a group of people round the back of the house next door, staring through the jalousie (a type of curtain). The neighbour said, 'What on earth is going on?'. The people told her that they could see an old woman running round and round the table. When the neighbour had a look, she

Mount Pleasant in 1905. Perhaps Mrs Gibbons lived on the left-hand side.

recognised Mrs Gibbons.

At another of the houses, the occupant arrived home one day to find Mrs Gibbons sitting in her living room. The occupant said, 'Well, Mrs Gibbons, where have you come from?' and with that, Mrs Gibbons put her arms forward and walked straight through the wall!

A third house was the first one past the Torrs. The occupants were in the bedroom one night and they could hear a commotion in the garden. It sounded as if a lot of animals had invaded. They could hear trampling noises and they could hear the bean sticks snapping in the night. The next morning they went out and everything was in place. Nothing had been touched.

There is no sign of Mrs Gibbons on the census returns for the second half of the nineteenth century but two ninety-year old residents remember the name.

Hide and seek
Headless Cross

As Mount Pleasant climbs away from Redditch it becomes the Evesham Road, where, in 1997, a student had a strange experience.

I have lived for about eight years in an old terraced house in Headless Cross which was built about 1890. About a couple of weeks ago I was upstairs, studying for my sociology examination, when I heard the door knocker go of our inner front door. We have an outer front door and an inner front door, both of which have frosted glass. The doors were closed and through them I could see the shape of a small person, like a child. I opened the inner door and was surprised to see that no-one was there. It had only taken me a fraction of a second to open it and I would have seen someone opening the outer door and leaving. I walked out through the inner door but when I opened the outer I felt as if someone rushed straight through me. It was like a ghostly wind, it didn't fill the doorway but only came to about hip height. In any case, this happened during a short warm, summery spell and so there was no real wind about. It doesn't seem logical but it was very real. Afterwards I felt really sick. I had to sit down and have a cup of tea.

On with the motley

The house in the next story is not far away and was built about the same time.

Our house is a Victorian end terrace. We moved here in 1990 and our two children were born here. The first thing that happened was that one afternoon, when I was working in

The trees of Pool Bank

the garden, I noticed my wife sitting in the kitchen. I didn't look properly, I could just see someone moving out of the corner of my eye. Then I remembered that my wife was at work, so when I went to see who it was, nobody was there.

Funny things happen. Things go missing, especially keys. We put all the keys on the rack at night and we say, 'Yes, there they are, all in a neat row', but when we get up in the morning they're gone. There will be one set on a cushion, another on a mat and in all sorts of strange places, such as drawers, where we never keep keys.

Whenever we have people to stay we put the guests in our own bedroom while we sleep on an inflatable bed downstairs. Often, our visitors complain that someone was hammering on the bedroom door at night but when they opened the door, no-one was there. This happened to my parents who came to stay one weekend. Both were woken up in the middle of the night by some really heavy banging on the bedroom door but when they opened the door no-one was there. That frightened them. It also happened to my brother-in-law who said that he was never going to stay here again. Those who baby sit say that they can hear a woman sobbing. It sounds as if it is downstairs but when they go outside to listen it isn't outside.

As soon as we moved here my little daughter began having nightmares about a clown.

We often wonder if it's anything to do with the fact that the lady previously living here committed suicide. She was a tiny lady, with frizzy hair dyed red and lots of make-up. She looked a bit like a clown.

The white lady of Pool Bank
(First published in the *Redditch Standard*)

Pool Bank Road runs downhill past the Quality Hotel and Torrs Close to Coldfield Drive. The Quality Hotel was once the home of the Terry family and so the woods which run along the southern edge of Pool Bank are known locally as 'Terry's Woods'. Often, those who walk alongside the woods complain that they felt they were being followed, but when they turned round no-one was there. The white lady of Pool Bank is a traditional Redditch ghost, said to be a young lady who hung herself in the woods at the turn of the century.

Late one evening in the winter of 1988, Tony had a terrifying experience.

Something happened to me in Pool Bank which was so scary that even now, many years later, I drive a long way round rather than go past that same spot at night.

At that time, I lived in Bromsgrove and my friends lived in Lodge Park. I used to go and see them regularly, at least once a week. The route took me along Pool Bank Road, into Mount Pleasant and down Plymouth Road. This one night at about eleven o'clock I was in my white MG Maestro and doing about forty or forty-five mph down Pool Bank Road. I know you're not supposed to go at that speed but it was a cold, clear night - not at all misty - and there was nobody about. All of a sudden this woman dressed in white suddenly appeared on my left. It all happened very quickly but I remember that she was a slim lady in a white cloak which was fairly loose and fell from the shoulders, and she had

73

either a very high collar or a hood. I saw her sideways on so that I could not see her face but she reminded me of the widow in the Scottish Widow's advertisement. She ran out of the woods and into the road right in front of me. I slammed on the brakes but she went under the car. There was no bump and this frightened me as much as anything.

I sat there for some minutes, too scared to get out. Although it was a cold night I should have been fairly warm in the car but I felt absolutely frozen. I still get the same feeling every time I go past the spot. Then I got out and looked under the car expecting to find someone lying there. To my surprise, the road was clear. It occurred to me that if it had been a real person she would have been halfway over the bonnet.

When I got home my wife asked, 'What's the matter with you?'. I told her that I had just seen a ghost and she laughed and said, 'You're as white as a ghost yourself!'. I said that she wouldn't be laughing if she'd just been through what I went through. I would emphasise that I had not been drinking.

Up to that point I had never believed in ghosts. I still don't really believe in ghosts but something ran across the road that night and there is no doubt that I hit it. It was most eerie. Now I say to people who say that they don't believe in ghosts, wait until you have seen something, then perhaps you will change your mind.

The resident apparition

Several of the large houses in the older parts of Redditch have been converted into residential homes. One of them is said to be haunted, a fact verified by an ex-employee.

Until recently, I worked nights at a residential home for the elderly. It was an old house which had been converted and it was a creepy place. Some women said that the atmosphere made them shudder and even the manager refused to stay there after dark. I was the only one who would work nights. I never saw anything strange but I often sensed that someone was watching me.

I have two teenage sons and occasionally, one or both of them would stay with me overnight. As the residents slept on the ground floor, we would sleep upstairs, putting large cushions on the floor as makeshift beds.

Every time my younger son came with me, something weird happened. He seemed to draw it. One night, just as I had tucked the last patient up in bed, all the alarm bells started ringing. I thought it was my son messing about and I thought, 'Wait till I get hold of him!'. I whispered up the stairs as loudly as I could, 'Will you stop messing about with these bells!' but as he looked over the banisters the bells were still ringing so that I knew that it wasn't him. When I was upstairs the bells seemed to be downstairs and when I was downstairs they seemed to be upstairs. I was quite panicky, wondering how to stop them but my son didn't seem a bit perturbed. He went back to watching the telly.

Another time, he was sitting watching the telly about nine or ten o'clock, when he saw a misty figure drift from the living room into the kitchen. Some months later he saw the transparent shape of a woman go from one room into the kitchen.

I was therefore quite surprised when, in 1995, it was not my younger but my older son who saw the apparition of a woman quite clearly. I was resting on the cushions on the floor when one of the buzzers went off so I got up and went out of the room. When I came back, he said, 'Who was that who followed you out?'. He had seen someone get up off the floor and follow me. He said that she was aged about thirty and slimmish. She was wearing a pill box hat and a black or dark blue lace dress with a high collar. Beneath the bodice was a bodystocking, and the underskirt was made of a stiffish fabric which made the skirt flare out from the waist, then drop straight to the floor. She had her back towards my son so he was not able to see her face.

We have been in the library looking in the costume books and we've found an outfit which is quite similar and dates to 1879. We have also been looking up in the records of the house to see if we can identify the ghost but we have had no luck so far.

The haunted pram
Crabbs Cross

During the second half of the nineteenth century and the beginning of the twentieth Crabbs Cross was dominated by a huge factory about half a mile away at Hunt End, used by Royal Enfield for about twenty years. At its height it could have employed up to a thousand workers. Many of them lived at Crabbs Cross and the Managing Director himself moved there in 1890. The factory has now disappeared but the social centre built for the workers still exists in the form of Samuel Latham's brush factory.

This lovely story is from a young lady living in Crabbs Cross with a three-year old daughter.

When I was pregnant my mother, who lives in King Norton, phoned me to tell me that she had found me a lovely second-hand pram. It was nearly new and it was a mint green MacLaren. My baby was twelve weeks premature and had to stay in hospital for almost five weeks after I went home, but my mother brought the pram over as soon as the baby was born so that it would be ready when I wanted to use it. During those five weeks that she was in hospital I could sometimes hear a baby crying, both during the day and at night.

When my baby came home I put the pram in the living room. Several times I heard a baby crying and I would go into the living room to see what the matter was and found her fast asleep. A couple of times I heard this baby screaming at about three o'clock in the morning. Her cot was in our bedroom so I got out of bed and had a look at her but, again, she was fast asleep. The noise seemed to be coming from the living room. I don't believe in anything like that but it really spooked me. I wouldn't put my baby in the pram and, after a few months, I gave the pram away to my husband's sister, and I didn't tell her why I was getting rid of it.

After she had had it a few weeks she told me that she was getting rid of the pram. She said that she could her a baby crying from whichever room she put it in. I told her then what had happened to me. Of course, this story got around to my mother's ears, and she told me that the reason that she had given the pram to me early in the first place was because she could hear this baby crying in it. That was the three of us had heard it and none of us had previously mentioned it to the other.

We wanted to know if there was any history to the pram but my mother had thrown away the address of the original owners of the pram, and only knew that the person she bought it from was quite young. I said to her, 'When you went to buy the pram, was there a child in the house?' and she said that there wasn't. That in itself seemed a bit strange to me. Why would a young woman have a pram if she had no children?

The Unicorn
Central Redditch

Right in the heart of Redditch, on the hill which bears its name, was the Unicorn Hotel. It has had a chequered history. In the nineteenth century it was a coaching inn, then it had a facelift when the new Redditch town was developed in the 1960's. Unfortunately, it acquired a poor reputation and when a life was lost during a disturbance in 1998, its licence was withdrawn and the building was demolished.

Young Marcus Bartlett was taken along as general helper and tea-maker.

I did some after-school work at Millsbro House and while I was there it was decided that the Unicorn Pub on Unicorn Hill would no longer be a public house, so my boss decided to buy it. I went along with one of the other bosses to help him.

One chap said that it was haunted and I thought they were just having me on. He was a bit of a practical joker. He told me that this one lady was a cleaner there and some years ago she put the story round that there was a grey lady who walked along the passage-way on the top floor.

The first time I was there I went into the Timber bar, so-called because of the Timber effects on the walls, to collect up the dirty cups. I put one cup down and just as I reached down to get another I saw, out of the corner of my eye, a cup slide about sixteen centimetres off the bar and smash on the floor. The bar was perfectly flat and there were no vibrations from the traffic.

The next time I went in (or a couple of times later) we had just finished for the day and were walking out of the building, locking up the door at the back, when we heard a loud bang. One of the bar hatches, which had been latched up, had slammed down. There was no reason why it should do this, it had been firmly clipped up and had remained clipped up for a couple of hours.

There were three bars altogether, you went down the back of the first bar through a door and a little passageway, down past a store cupboard and on to another bar. There were three of us, me and a couple of blokes. I was the last. The place was in darkness as all the shutters were up. As we walked along you could hear the noise of light bulbs falling and hitting the floor and popping. We shone the torch up from where the bulbs had fallen, but there were no light fittings on the ceiling. There was glass everywhere. About six or seven bulbs had fallen and smashed on the floor and there were only three light fittings in the whole ceiling. I was kneeling down, sweeping up the broken glass by the light of two large builders' spotlights when something literally threw a pint glass at me. It just hit me from the front and the glass fell to the floor and smashed.

Another curious fact that we never managed to understand was that on one of the walls of one of the rooms at the front was a complete mirror image of the building over the road but it was upside down. You could even see the people walking past. This image seemed to be shining through a crack but why should it be upside down? We never had time to investigate properly.

I wouldn't go back into the building after that. People were trying to get me to go in again but I wouldn't. I only returned when it was partly demolished to take some photographs. All the time I was there I had a cold, damp feeling and I felt as if someone was watching me.

The Unicorn Hotel and, opposite page, the Unicorn sculpture which has been retained.

Fire burn and cauldron bubble

Before the new town was built, the old road from Redditch to Birmingham ran past the Fire Station. Only a quarter of a mile away are the ancient meadows of Bordesley Abbey. Fire Stations seem particularly susceptible to these strange vibes. The haunting at Pershore Fire Station has already been mentioned. In *Midland Ghosts and Hauntings* we describe the manifestations at Perry Common in Birmingham. Smethwick Fire station was believed to be haunted by the ghost of Captain Thomas Chandler who committed suicide at the station in 1923.

During the early 1990's there was a rumour circulating round Redditch that the local fire station was haunted. Strange, inexplicable breezes would suddenly blow in certain areas and a ghostly monk was seen. Then, apparently, these strange manifestations stopped and were later referred to as a joke.

Towards the end of 1996 the road outside the Fire Station was widened and the traffic lights were installed. The dormitory, where the Firemen slept, was on the ground floor right next to the road-widening scheme so the sleeping quarters had to be moved to another part of the station. While the old dormitory was empty, it was decided that it should be upgraded.

The work on the dormitory seems to have disturbed whatever was in the brickwork. The strange manifestations returned. There are four watches and someone from all different watches either experienced the cold breeze or saw the outline of a dark figure.

In January 1997 one of the Firemen had an experience which frightened him more that anything he had come across in the course of his work:

> In the early hours of the morning I was woken up by a cold blast of air. I looked up and hovering above me, only a few feet away, was a large dark shadow. I tried to shout out, but my mouth would not move. I tried to jump out of bed but I felt as if I were being held by an invisible force. I was terrified.

The doppelganger
Millsbro Road

Very occasionally, an example of the doppelganger phenomenon occurs. The word comes from German folklore, where a doppelganger was a mythical beast who followed a person round for a long period and eventually took over his or her personality. It is now used more loosely and usually refers to one's double. Fortunately, to see one's double is a very rare occurrence because it was once thought to be a 'death token', ie to foretell ones death, as in the following anecdote. It comes from the William Avery's collection of *Redditch Indicator* clippings which was completed in 1906:

> Near the same spot (Beoley) Mr William Guardner saw his own "death token" a week or so before he fell off a hay rick and died in consequence of the fall. Crossing the fields homewards on a fine summer's evening, he was surprised to see before him a man exactly resembling himself in dress and figure, in short, "a double." He hurried on to

overtake his later ego, but in vain; the apparition kept before him at the same distance, and on coming to the stile leading into the Watery Lane, vanished. Mr Guardner related the occurrence when he reached home and shortly afterwards met with the accident which caused his death

During her lifetime Lisa Greenwood* has had a number of strange experiences - she lived in a house where there was some mild poltergeist activity and she has the occasional premonition. Then early in 1998 ...

> ... a peculiar thing happened to me. My son was at the 'Workshop Studios' in Millsbro Road, Redditch, with his band. I had to go and pick him up when he'd finished. It was about ten thirty at night. The door to the studio is in Millsbro Road and when you park outside the door you are on a camera and everyone inside can see you. That night I stopped the car outside the door, I was the only one there. It was raining quite hard so I decided to sit in the car and wait instead of getting out and pushing the button on the door. I knew they would know I was there as they would have seen me on the camera. When my son came out he said, 'Why didn't you come in?'. I replied that as it was raining I thought that I would stay in the car. My son then said, 'But you came and stood by the door'. They had all watched me get out of the car and stand by the door. My son said that it was definitely me as the person had exactly the same clothes as I had got on. It really made the hairs stand up on the back of my neck when he told me. How would you explain that they saw me standing there when I didn't even get out of the car?

We're happy to report that Lisa remains in good health.

Immortal spirit

In April 1964, Redditch was designated a New Town. Over the next twenty years the population rose from 35,860 to 70,000. Redditch is very much a new town, and the remainder of the Redditch stories are from people with new houses which were built on wasteland or farmland.

Susan* and her brother were very close and she was devastated when he died from leukaemia in 1986.

> He was at home the day that he died, I went to see him and he made me a cup of coffee but I felt as if I were looking at him through glass and I couldn't touch him. Late that evening, I was in bed reading, when suddenly I heard this choir, a rich beautiful sound with no words, it sounded as if they were laa-ing. It was very, very real. If a choir were singing at a memorial service that's the kind of sound they would make. I thought that my sons must have left the television on but they hadn't. Then I thought it must be a radio but I was a bit surprised because it wasn't the kind of music they would listen to. But there was no radio left on. I opened the front door and listened and I could still hear the music, then I went back to bed and I could still hear it, at just the same volume. It seemed to have

79

no source. He died at eleven o'clock that evening.

One evening, about six weeks after he died I was at the sink when I just turned round and there he was. He appeared to be in the garden of his own house, looking at me through the smaller of his lounge windows. He was superimposed over the corner of my room. He looked like a colour slide in the corner of the kitchen or as if he was on video but there was no frame. He wasn't transparent, like a ghost, but I knew that I couldn't touch him. He stifled a laugh - he got that from my mother - where his shoulder would shake and his face would grin but he would not make any sound. I know why he was laughing, we often talked about life before and after death and he was giving me an example. He was wearing a Fair Isle pullover. I mentioned to his wife later that I had seen him and she asked me if I would know the pullover again. She went upstairs and brought down a Fair Isle pullover, and I recognised it straight away. She said that she knitted it for him some years previously but he very rarely wore it. She knew that I had never seen it before.

The second time I saw him he seemed to be on holiday. Again, I was working at the sink in the kitchen and I turned round and there he was, looking as if he was on film. He was wearing beige trousers and a blue checked shirt and he was outside a long white building, like a villa, with arches and stuccoed walls, and there was a beach a long way down. He went inside the villa (which was a restaurant or something) and then everything became jumbled up like a dream and it all crumbled away. Again, his wife asked me if I would recognise the clothes. He had several pairs of beige trousers and more than one checked shirt. His wife kept going upstairs and bringing them down and to each one I said, 'No, that wasn't quite the right colour'. Finally I was able to say yes, those were the ones. I was very glad that I had been able to find the right clothes. I could prove that what I had seen wasn't just my imagination.

I described the building to my sister-in-law but she couldn't remember staying in a holiday home like that. Anyway, a few months later I was looking through some old photographs and there was the building. I said to my sister-in-law, 'This is it!'. She said that she had forgotten about that holiday which was on a Spanish island. Seeing that photograph knocked me for six. It was as if my brother had organised the whole thing.

On the last occasion that I saw him I was at a Yoga class. We were just relaxing, I closed my eyes and I saw him in my mind's eye. He was wearing a dark blue or black uniform with red piping and a peaked cap and he seemed to be superimposed over a Nissan hut. It didn't mean anything to me then but I found out later that he had been in the military police. My brother in America also saw him in the military police uniform and we worked out afterwards that it must have been about the same time. He's a bit confused as he doesn't believe in anything like that.

The Avon lady apparition
Callow Hill

Over the last fifteen years Callow Hill Village has spread through the rural backwaters of Worcestershire, two miles south west of Redditch. This is one of the desirable areas, with detached dwellings only. Margaret Johnson* lives in a bungalow at the end of one of these quiet roads.

> I never buy anything from the Avon lady as I'm allergic to some of their products and I was surprised to find, one day last year, that one of their catalogues had been pushed through my door. I put it back outside the front door on the day that the lady was due to come, as requested in the catalogue. That afternoon I was working hard so I thought, 'I'll sit down for five minutes'. I was in the easy chair in front of the lounge window when I saw this old lady stride past the window and up to the front door. She was wearing a blue pinafore skirt with a square neck and a white short-sleeved jumper underneath. Her hair was quite short and it was the kind of grey from which you could tell that her hair had once been dark. I could see her head and shoulders above the window ledge and I would judge that she was about five feet six inches tall. There was nothing unusual about her except that she had a hump on the one shoulder.
>
> She looked very purposeful and I assumed she had come to collect the catalogue. I thought, 'Fancy sending that old lady to collect it!'. It is very quiet here, there is no traffic and I realised that I hadn't heard a car. I said to myself, 'Poor old dear, has she walked here?' and I opened the door and looked out and up and down the road. The Avon catalogue was still on the step and the old lady was not to be seen. There's nowhere she could have gone, our garage doors were closed and there's a blank wall on each side of our house. Without any doubt I saw her going up to our front door and it only took me a second or two to get to the door. I went straight away and I'm pretty quick off my feet. She couldn't have gone anywhere.
>
> I wasn't scared at the time but afterwards, when I thought about it, the hairs stood up on the back of my neck.

The ghost train
Greenlands

Newcomers to Studley village may wonder why the far end of the High Street is named Station Road, when the nearest station is at least three miles away in Redditch. The reason is that a delightful twisting single track once ran from Redditch, through Studley, all the way to Evesham. Studley Station was on the Slough, next to Green Lane. The line was closed in June 1964.

In WB Herbert's book, *Railway Ghosts and Phantoms* (published by David & Charles in 1989), Mr Bernard Essex of Studley describes how he heard a phantom steam train at six o'clock in the morning. He opened the window for a clearer sound and without doubt heard the noise of a steam train approaching, reaching a crescendo and dying away. The line had closed three months previously and the track was still in situ but all the point and controls had been removed.

A more recent sighting, or rather hearing, comes from Linda who lives on the south-eastern side of Redditch, near the Throckmorton Road in Greenlands.

I had been living in Greenlands with my second husband for five months when this happened. I remember the date, Monday, 12th October 1998 because the next day I was due in court over a custody battle concerning my children by my first marriage.

It was late at night and I was just dropping off to sleep when I heard this strange noise. I said to my husband, 'Can you hear that?'. It sounded just like a steam train coming nearer and going past, then it went whoo-oo and seemed to go into a tunnel. My husband heard it too.

I made enquiries and apparently, the line from Studley ran close by, past the hospital and near to where MacDonalds is now. Then it went into the tunnel, which is now Tunnel Drive, by B & Q. We have been told that it used to hoot just before it went into the tunnel. That is what I heard. It was definitely a train and definitely a steam train. It was nice but a bit eerie.

Life with a dark shape
Matchborough

Further to the east from Greenlands is Matchborough. These estates were planned to be self-sufficient and Matchborough centre has shops, a church, a pub and a meeting place. The next story comes from Matchborough East. The house was built in 1972 and David Price* moved into it only a few years later. He raised his family there before he moved out in 1990, but he noticed strange things happening for two or three years before he left.

All kinds of common little things used to disappear - especially tools. I do a lot of work at home, and I would put some tool down, go out of the room for a minute and when I came back I wouldn't be able to find it. Then some time later, I would be just sitting there at my bench and the tool would be there, exactly where I left it.

My wife and I used to sit and watch TV at night, leaving the lounge door open so that we could hear the kids, which meant that we could see into the corridor and part of the open plan staircase. Something would catch my attention through the corner of my eye. I discovered that if I looked just off-centre from my eye I could see a grey shape, but if I looked straight at the shape, it would disappear. It was just a vertical grey blur, you couldn't make out whether it was male or female. It was about as tall as a short person and would move at about the speed of an someone elderly. The odd thing was that it always seemed to be gliding up the stairs, never down.

I tended to think that this was my imagination, but things came to a head one evening when I was looking sideways at this shape and my wife said, 'What are you doing?'. I didn't want to alarm her, so I answered 'Nothing!'. She said, 'You are, you're looking sideways'. I tried to think of some excuse and she said, 'You can see it too, can't you?'. It turned out that she had always been seeing this shape. My wife reckoned it was her mother, who was an extremely nice person, but I think we had had this shape for a good twelve months before her mother died. However, one incident that I would mention was that not long after she had died, my one lad, then aged about ten or eleven, came in and said, 'Nan was here again last night'. I asked him what he meant and I said, 'Did you see her?'. My son said that he hadn't but that he had smelt her as she used this very distinctive perfume.

The shape appeared most evenings, but it was not at all frightening and it didn't stop us going up the stairs. There were no bumps or bangs or anything like that and no feeling of evil. We reckoned that whatever it was could only be friendly and when we left we invited the shape to go with us, but it didn't.

The psychic wife
Winyates

Going north from Matchborough we come to Winyates, which is just over a mile east of Redditch. Both Matchborough and Winyates gave the builders of the housing estates quite a headache as the soil tends to be a heavy red clay. Perhaps it was this red clay which gave Red-ditch its name.

What is it like to be married to someone who appears to have some kind of psychic ability? Adrian Fellows* has a few unusual anecdotes to tell about his wife, Marian*.

I'm very sceptical about the paranormal, I wouldn't say I was a believer but I must admit that some strange things go on in our household. My wife, Marian, seems to be a bit psychic - let me tell you about a couple of incidents which happened recently.

83

Early in 1966 she kept saying to me, 'Do be careful' and she told me that she had had a vision of a police officer coming towards her. He was dressed in yellow, like a traffic warden and although he approached her, it was me that he wanted. She kept on about this, then about two months later, she opened the door one evening to find the police officer of her vision standing there asking for me. I had been involved in a minor accident, someone had reported me and the officer had come to breathalyse me. Fortunately the case never reached court but it was all very unpleasant and we had to see a solicitor to sort things out.

In the summer she told me that I was going to come into some money - just a small amount. I said to her, 'Do I win it?'. She said not. 'Do I earn it?'. Again, she said not. 'Do I inherit it?' Again, no. I said to her, 'How am I going to get hold of it then?' She replied that she didn't know. Two weeks later, in June, I had an income tax rebate for £46.

These predictions are not the only unusual things to happen in our house. Things go missing, especially clothes. A pair of my jeans went missing for a whole week. I was desperate for them and turned the whole house upside down. I looked everywhere, even the airing cupboard. Then a week later, I opened my wardrobe door and there they were, right at the front. It was impossible for them to have been there before, we had both searched through the wardrobe the day that they went missing and the following day. The question is, where did they go? How could they disappear into thin air?

A week or two ago I was sitting downstairs when everyone else had gone to bed. The kitchen cupboard has a plastic latch which clicks and I suddenly heard this latch click and a noise as if someone was putting a plate on the side. We live with my in-laws and I assumed that my father-in-law had gone downstairs and was helping himself to a late snack, so with the thought of food in mind I went into the kitchen. No more than ten seconds had elapsed but no-one was there and nothing had been moved. I know without a doubt that I heard that noise and I thought that someone was playing a joke, but everyone denied it and in any case, they were all in bed.

Marian is a smartly-dressed professional woman in her early thirties, articulate and intelligent.

I'm a natural psychic. When I was small my parents were quite worried about me because I used to see things and know things that I shouldn't know. I used to see a dog and even feed it. I would make comments about things that happened in the past before I was born that I shouldn't know about. They even took me to see a doctor.

We didn't move to Redditch until I was about eleven, before that I lived in Birmingham. When I was about eight or nine I went to my brother's room to get a game, and as I went in the door slammed behind me. It was an awkward door and wouldn't close, so it was very strange for it to slam. I tried to open the door but it wouldn't open. I turned back round to see the curtains in the room going up and down as if they had been caught in a gale, then the cupboard doors opened and all the toys and games in the cupboard just flew out. I was knocking at the door and shouting, it was an awful row. My mother came upstairs in a real temper. She opened the door with no problem and of course I had a slap for making such a mess.

Then as I got older and reached puberty things really started to happen and I had a lot of problems. My friends and I did something stupid, we devised a Ouija board at school and I picked something up from that. It was a man, he came back home with me and created a lot of disturbances. All my clothes would just suddenly be pulled off the hangers and thrown about. There was an awful lot of tension and a lot of banging. At certain times and especially at three o'clock in the morning, he would hammer on my bedroom door. Eventually that fizzled out. A lot of it was my fault. You can bring in your own energy and frustration and channel it out.

A few years later I started using the Tarot cards and I found they were a good key for me. I don't usually read the symbolism, I use them more as a key, and people like you to have something in front of you when you make predictions, it puts them at ease. As far as I know, everything that I have said has come true, I have never predicted something that wasn't correct.

I don't really enjoy being psychic. I often wonder if I am going mad. In 1995 I lost my dog and about three months later my husband and I heard her scratching and crying at the bedroom door. For about a month recently we were having people calling my name. I would say to the family, 'Well, what do you want?' and they would say that they hadn't said anything. There was another spate where doors were being banged and items, especially clothing, disappeared. My watch went missing for four days and turned up in the middle of the bedroom floor.

On the other hand, I find that I can sense things about people, it makes you aware of people's personalities. I'm good at weighing people up quickly, I've never found that I was wrong, and, as I work with people, it is a great help in my profession. However, I don't tell anyone about this, my colleagues might think that I was weird and this would get in the way of my job prospects.

A fair maid dwellin'
Church Hill

Going north again and crossing the Coventry Highway we reach Church Hill. The site of a Roman road runs through the centre, and to the west are the Bordesley Abbey meadows, to the north is Beoley with its ancient church and sinister reputation (see *Haunted Worcestershire*). To the east is Moon's Moat, now chiefly an industrial estate but at one time a lonely, marshy place. Lady Moon (or Mohun) is said to walk on the eve of Saint Agnes (January 21st). The Moon family lived in a moated grange here but they had died out by the middle of the eighteenth century.

Marlfield farm once stood in Church Hill North but was demolished in 1977. The barn was built by the Bomford family in traditional style, using old timbers, in1925 as a cowshed and is still standing. It was reconstructed as a recreational centre between 1960 and 1983. The new First School is

85

named after the farm.

The locals tell the story that when Mrs Leeming was headmistress, her father, Mr Smith, came to visit the school. Before he retired he had been a police inspector or something like that. Anyway, he was parking his car in the parking area when he saw this young woman walking towards the bushes. She was wearing a brown cloak with a cowl and was carrying a three-legged stool. He lost sight of her when she went behind a bush. He jumped out of his car and looked all round but there was no sign of any-one. She couldn't have gone anywhere because there was a thick hedge all round.

When he went into the school his daughter said to him, 'What is the matter? You look terrible!' and he replied 'I think I have just seen a ghost'. He drew a picture of the lady and pinned it up in the staff room hoping someone would come up with an explanation, but nobody did.

Two years later, during the long summer holidays, some work was being done on the suspended ceiling in the staff room. One of the workmen was up a ladder, trying to repair the ceiling. The staffroom door was open so that he could see up the corridor as far as the secretary's office. Suddenly he noticed a nun in the corridor walking into the hall. He scrambled down the ladder and rushed to the hall and was just going to tell her that the school was closed when she walked through the wall. The workman was so fright-ened that he wouldn't go back to finish the job.

These incidents happened ten years ago or more, well before the children now at the school were born. No further incidents have been reported since.

What the Shannanigans!
Church Hill

Many of the ghost stories in this book suggest poltergeist activity and the following is a classic poltergeist scenario. An interesting fact is that the nar-rator was seriously ill with cancer at that time but did not know this until after the following events.

> The memory of the following events is still vivid even though they happened some years ago, to be precise over a period of five years between 1981 and 1986. Towards 1986 they got worse when my daughter and I noticed more things happening.

I think I am slightly psychic, I often think of someone and at that moment the telephone rings and that person is on the other end of the line. I can often sense people's feelings, which has proved quite invaluable in my professional career. An acquaintance once told me that I could read her thought patterns.

This was a new house when my daughter, Charlotte*, and I moved here in 1974. Charlotte didn't want to move here and I must admit that I always felt that something was watching me as I went from the lounge door to the bottom of the stairs. Charlotte was the same. This scared me quite a lot, whenever I had to go upstairs I would always dread coming back down again.

I have thought a great deal about what could have caused the following events and I can find no rational explanation. When they began Charlotte was ten and I had just started a degree course at college. My daughter knew that if, at any time, the college course was a problem I would abandon it. My next door neighbour kept an eye on her whenever she was in the house alone but often we arrived home together. Charlotte kept diaries in which she put all her thoughts, we have looked through these and the overall picture is of a little girl with a happy life.

Only one thing comes to mind - in 1981 my stepfather died. He and Charlotte were very close and she always had a remarkable effect on him. For example, he had a stroke a couple of months before he died and was very poorly but when she walked into the hospital ward it was almost like a miracle. He sat up in bed and put his arms out to her. The doctor called the nursing staff to see it. It was not long after he died that these things began to happen.

First of all we noticed that the letter box used to clatter as if the post had just come through. One or other of us would dash to get the post and there would be nothing there. Our friends who used to visit us would hear this too. It was very regular, several times a week and sometimes in the evening, this was not unusual as the *Advertiser* and other local papers arrived in the evening. I got the letter box changed but it still rattled.

Early one morning about six to six-thirty, I heard this sudden thud. The thought came to my head that Charlotte had fallen out of bed. I rushed to her room but she was sound asleep. I shook her to see if she was alright. She wasn't very pleased and said, 'What have you woken me up for?'. It sounded like a body falling and as I had an elderly neighbour I thought that perhaps she had had a fall or dropped something and I called to see if she was OK but there was nothing wrong. I was not asleep at the time and I wasn't dreaming. This happened three or four times early on in 1981 but with quite an interval in between. I would just have forgotten about the incident and it would happen again.

Charlotte loved music and would put a tape on and sing and dance away to her heart's content. Then she would hear someone knock at the door so she would stop and look through the letter box but no-one would be there nor going away towards the garden gate.

Although my next door neighbour was quite elderly she was very astute and articulate. She would say things like 'Your daughter's having boys round at the house' and she told me that a very blond boy used to come to the house quite regularly and look through the letter box. The next door neighbour constantly talked about him. I knew who Charlotte's friends were, no-one answered that description, and if she had anybody here she would tell me. My daughter wasn't interested in boys anyway, she was not that way inclined. Charlotte laughed at me when I told her and added that the old lady must be imagining things.

Things used to go missing. I had to fill up the sugar bowl more and more frequently, we would get through two packets a week whereas normally one would last us a month. The level of the marmalade would go down at a terrific rate and the same with the tea bags which were kept in a box. . I used to say to Charlotte, it's not good for you to eat the sugar and the marmalade like this. She used to protest that it wasn't her and in case, she didn't like sugar and marmalade! I still don't understand how it is possible for store cupboard items such as sugar, marmalade and tea bags to go missing. Where would they go? To this day I cannot understand it. Sometimes I used to wonder if there wasn't someone else living here when I was out.

I used to have a twin tub washing machine. It was fairly heavy and quite an exercise to get it under the unit. About twice a week I used to come home and it would be askew, and well into the kitchen. I would say to Charlotte, this isn't a toy, you mustn't play with it. She would insist that she hadn't touched it. I actually did reprimand my daughter for a lot of the happenings in the early days, and sometimes she ended up in tears. She wasn't a naughty girl, I could leave things about and know that she could be trusted. Then as she began to tell me about things that were happening to her I started to think otherwise and suspect that perhaps something extraordinary was happening. At first I was a little bit curious. I began to wonder, too, if I was imagining things, if something was happening to my mind but as I had no difficulty coping with the degree course I thought that this couldn't be so.

It makes me shudder to think of the times that I have sat in the lounge, felt a cold chill and heard someone come through the door. I used to work in the lounge until quite late into the night and several times the room would go terribly cold and I felt as if someone had tapped me on the shoulder. I would think that Charlotte had crept downstairs but she was always fast asleep in bed.

Several times a week I would go off to bed switching off the lights and come downstairs in the morning to find some of them on. I have a ceiling light which I don't use very often and this would be on. I thought maybe one of us was sleepwalking so I decided to stay awake all night. I thought that if I sat up all night and then, in the morning, if a light was on or something was missing I would know that it was neither of us.

I have often come home after having been out, certain I had locked the door and the door would be unlocked. Yet the lock was never forced. No-one else had the key to the house, only Charlotte. I would think, 'Next time I lock up I must be more careful'. Each time something happened I made a more conscious effort to put the lights out or lock the doors. I would double check. However, I have lived on my own for many years and I am used to making sure that everything is alright.

One of the first things that I do when I come into the house is to take my ring and watch off and put them in one of two places. The ring is more sentimental value than anything. I lost it for four days, then I found it in a toilet bag right at the back of the cabinet in the bathroom. I cannot understand how it got there. I only use it when on holiday and we hadn't been away for quite some time!

I once found myself locked inside the house. Charlotte had gone to school and I went to get my keys from the normal spot and they weren't there. I thought maybe I had put them somewhere else and I searched through everything which wasn't too difficult as in those days I didn't have lots of cupboards and drawers. In the finish I phoned up the school and asked if Charlotte had taken my keys as well as her own. She hadn't and one of the teachers brought her home to let me out. It was very embarrassing. The keys were later found neatly placed on top of the jumper on my bedroom chair. Charlotte and I had both shaken the jumper.

On many occasions, we would be safely tucked up in bed at night and it would sound as if there was somebody in my kitchen. I would hear the light click on, cupboards would click open, it would sound as if the kettle was being switched on and things were being pulled out of cupboards. At first, I had a tendency to dismiss these things, to pretend that they weren't happening. Then I would hear footsteps slowly coming up the stairs. Our stairs were not carpeted and I could hear the foot-steps on the wood. They were fairly slow and quite heavy, perhaps that of a man? There was one day when I was in the bath and I heard these footsteps coming up the stairs. I assumed I had accidentally left the front door unlocked and somebody had come into the house, I was so scared! I locked the bathroom door. I shouted down, 'Whoever you are, b... off!', and later I came downstairs but the door was still locked. I have now had my locks changed, just in case.

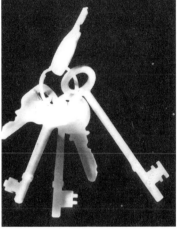

Occasionally I would see an image in my room, just a shadow. The image would walk around my bed to the other side of the bed where I sleep and sit in my bed. I was petrified, I didn't know what to do. My bedroom was the one place where I thought I was safe! I put a bible by my bed. I didn't tell my daughter because I didn't want her to be frightened.

One night I was lying in bed and I definitely wasn't asleep, and I am certain that this wasn't a dream. My heart was pounding like hell - I heard footsteps very clearly because there were wooden stairs and there was no mistaking somebody clomping up the stairs. I was pretending to be asleep but I just peeped round the bedclothes. I heard the bed-room door open. I was so scared. I could just see this figure which filled the doorway. Somebody was standing looking at me. The whole figure was very dark and he had pageboy style of hair, longish and black. As for his clothes - he wore a tunic-type top. I think he had some long boots on. I can't remember the colourings of the clothes, I can only remember the style. I can remember peeping and thinking, 'If he has come to burgle he can take whatever he likes but just leave me alone'. I don't suppose he was standing there for very long but at the time it seemed ages. I was too scared to scream out. I thought somebody had broken into the house and was coming to harm me. The only thing I could do is just go along with it. Where my bed is placed he walked up to it and round and I felt him sit on my bed. I don't know how my heart didn't stop. Then he actually got into my bed. I was lying on my side and he lay behind me and put his arms round me and performed. I thought, 'If I scream he may hurt me'.

Then he wanted more but I said, 'Let's get some sleep now' or something like that. He was very gentle, not rough or anything. I don't remember much more after that. I must have fallen asleep and when I woke up there was nobody there. I can remember looking round the house to see if anything had been taken but there was nobody there, nothing had gone and the house was still all locked. My small daughter was sleeping in the room next door.

I began to wonder if I was working too hard, under a great deal of stress, but I have the reputation of coping well with stress. As things rapidly got worse I became very frightened but I would try to put it out of my mind and each time I was able to dismiss it until the next incident.

The last straw came when I was in the bathroom, and the light cord started to swing really violently from side to side as if someone had knocked it. I was out of the bath and downstairs as quickly as anything. I thought, 'We have got to move, I can't stand this!' and I decided that I needed professional help. I spoke to some of my friends and I was given the telephone number of someone to contact. A lady and two men came out, the men said that they would go through room by room and I must move out of whatever room they were in. While they were in my bedroom there was a tremendous commotion and a loud bang. It sounded as if there was going to be a great mess but when I went upstairs nothing was out of place. They came down and said, 'It's alright now'. They told me that there was a presence in my bedroom, and I had thought myself safe in there!'.

A few days after the spiritualists had been to the house, a figure floated past my bed. I didn't see it so clearly this time, only a shadow and it was not so tall. It was if he was saying, 'I only came to say good-bye'.

Certainly something occurred here that was unusual but very little has happened since and I now feel quite comfortable living here.

Charlotte now lives in Birmingham from where she sends a letter confirming these incidents and adding:

I never actually saw anything, and in fact got the blame for many of the events - like the sugar disappearing and the old twin tub being moved - and I can honestly say that I never touched these things. I think my mother started to believe that it was something of the paranormal when she lost her keys, and was locked in the house - she searched high and low, and in the end had to call me from school. When I arrived home with my teacher we continued the search but to no avail, and so left the house. When we returned, my mother went into her room and shrieked that she had found her keys - they were lying on top of her jumper on her chair in the corner of the room. I can quite distinctly remember her shaking her jumper fiercely in our earlier search - and now they were placed neatly on top.

TENBURY WELLS

efore the nineteenth century Tenbury was merely a coaching town on one of the main roads from London to North Wales. Then in 1839, mineral springs were discovered, a pump room was built and the word 'Wells' added to the name. Nikolaus Pevsner, in his book on Worcestershire writes, 'For a while the little town flourished but it soon sank back into its comfortable tranquillity'. The bizarre pagoda-shaped building erected to house the water-cure facilities still exists behind the Crow Hotel.

Buried treasure

Opposite the great Victorian church of St Mary's (rebuilt in 1865) in the heart of Tenbury is a row of picturesque old cottages. One of them, until recently, was occupied by Jim Bailey who says:

I have always lived in interesting houses, the older the better. At the beginning of the last war I lived in a large Victorian terraced house with my parents. They told me the following story many times.

Before the days of television card-playing was very popular, and my parents used to stop up most of the night playing cards. Sometimes they used to go to bed leaving the cards out on the table. When they got up in the morning the cards would be scattered all over the floor. They also heard strange noises during the night, as if furniture was being moved.

One morning, they went downstairs to find a trail of coal leading from the bottom of the stairs to the cellar, and coal had been taken out of the cellar. A few years later they had some alterations made to the house which meant that the hall floor had to be dug up. There, where the coal trail had ended, was a wooden box, about one-and-a-half feet by nine inches, and nine inches deep. When they opened it they found it was full of old coins. It was as if something had been trying to show them where the treasure was buried.

Unfortunately, when they took their treasure to the bank, the officials said that the coins were out of date and not cashable. I don't know what happened to them in the end.

Have you heard about the ghost?

Saint Michael's, the Roman Catholic church, is the older church by nine years. The following incident, told by a member of the Tenbury Wells and District Civic and Historical Society, took place outside the church hall in 1997.

Sometime after Easter my wife and I were at a function at the church hall. Knowing I was a church member, a lady said to me, 'Did you have a service at the Church on Good Friday?'. I replied, 'Oh no, we never do'. Then this lady said to me, 'My friend and I saw a monk standing at the side of the road. We thought it was a prank and we didn't think anything about it'. A few weeks later my wife was at a meeting with some of her friends and they said, 'Have you heard about this ghost?'. Another of her friends said, 'I have seen it, it's a tall monk in a brown cowl and brown habit'. She had seen it virtually in the same place when she was driving past. We asked her if she stopped and she replied no, she was too frightened.

My friend's son sometimes goes round that area taking the dog out. He has never seen anything but on one occasion the dog's hairs stood up on end and he froze.

Enquiries at Saint Michaels and in Tenbury Wells failed to throw any light on the matter.

Opposite page: Saint Mary's Church, Tenbury Wells

The valley of the shadow of death

There are few stories more tragic than the next.

For most of my life I have had a very dear friend and although she no longer lives in Tenbury we still keep in touch. She is older than I am but we seem to have a kind of mental rapport, almost a telepathic link Often, a few months go by and I think, I must get in touch with Margaret*, then the phone rings and at the same moment, she has called me.

While she was living close by she had a small daughter, Jane. I almost lived at Margaret's house. I became a kind of older sister to the little girl, we would play games together and I was only too happy to baby mind whenever I was asked. When she was five she was taken ill, I helped to nurse her, but it turned out to be meningitis and she died. I always remember, after the funeral, her father saying, 'At least I won't have to chase the boys away when she's seventeen'. I thought that was the most poignant remark I had ever heard.

About seven years later I myself had a little girl. When my daughter was aged about five I woke up in the middle of the night and there, at the end of my bed, was Jane, but not as I knew her but older, aged about seventeen. She just stood there, as clearly as if it were daylight, with her arms outstretched. Slowly, she came towards me but as she came nearer she faded away.

My own daughter died from cancer when she was seventeen. I often think about that apparition. Did I pick up some telepathic image from my friend, Margaret, or was the apparition genuine? If so, why did it pay me a visit? Was it a warning of some kind? Was it to tell me that death is not final and she was alright?

UPTON-ON-SEVERN

pton-on-Severn was once a busy inland port, with the only bridge between Worcester and Gloucester where you could cross the Severn. It was also on the junction of several main roads and still has several handsome Georgian inns. The town was so prosperous that it was able to build a new parish church three times. The first stone Church was built close to the Severn in the fourteenth century. In the middle of the 1700's this first church was pulled down and rebuilt, all except for the tower, which was crowned by two decorative dome-shaped structures, a smaller one (a lantern) on top of a larger one. This second church was again abandoned when a completely new church was built at the west end of the town in 1879. Again, the fourteenth century tower was left standing and is still there, complete with its unusual crown, known affectionately by the locals as 'The Pepperpot'.

The pepperpot urchin

Only a stones' throw from this tower is a row of ancient houses probably dating back to the sixteenth century. A young couple, *Rob and *Maria, moved into one of them in the autumn of 1997. Maria says that it was early evening

and they were still unpacking when the first unusual incident occurred.

A friend and her sister were helping us to unpack. This friend came downstairs and went into the kitchen and she was amazed to see a plate fly out of the cupboard, hover a bit then smash onto the floor, breaking into pieces. Later, the friend and her sister went home, and then I discovered that I could see this dark shape of a child bobbing about, playing hide and seek. I wasn't at all afraid, I thought it was quite funny.

On the first night I woke up with the feeling that somebody was in the room. I looked at the door and saw this dark shape coming through. I asked her who she was but her replies were very vague. I gathered she was about seven years old.

I have seen her regularly since, sometimes quite clearly. She has fair or auburn hair, red cheeks and a thinnish face. She's wearing a white pinafore with lace round the bottom over a dark Victorian dress with leg-of-mutton sleeves and a high v-neck edged with white lace.

Rob also sees her regularly and says:

I first saw her when I was emptying the ashes a couple of days after we moved in. I was scraping them out and she was standing there, I could just see the outline of a shadow. A few days later I was drinking a glass of wine when something seemed to go 'wham!' at the glass and the wine shot all over me.

About a month later, I was sitting in the living room when I saw her walking through from the kitchen to the living room. I looked twice in case my eyes were playing tricks. Although she was only a shadow, I could see her clearly enough to pick out the details and see what she was wearing. Her face was set in the one direction as if she was walking towards somebody.

She now visits us more and more often. She seems to like to watch me emptying the ashes and she often appears then. We frequently pick her up on the landing - sometimes we see her but usually it's just that as we open a bedroom door the bathroom door will move as if she is opening it for you. She loves our two cats and we sometimes see her bending over them. Each time we see her she has become clearer and clearer.

I last saw her about a week ago when I was sitting in the living room watching TV. One of the cats darted across the room and so I turned to see what had startled the cat. I saw her standing in the kitchen doorway, very faint but clear enough to pick out what she was wearing.

A final word comes from Maria:

The last time I saw her was about two weeks ago, when she came into my bedroom. She was standing there, leaning over me, for about five or ten minutes. In the end I said to her, 'Would you please go away and play now, I want to go to sleep', and she went. One or other of us sees her almost every day. We usually know when she's going to put in an appearance because the candelabra starts to swing and she startles the cats, they fly from one room to the other.

We have no idea who she is. We have asked our elderly neighbours but, as far as they know, there has been no tragic death nor any other misfortune to a young child

A family tragedy

A housewife who once lived in Upton-on-Severn likes to keep in touch and has the *Upton News* passed to her by a friend. On looking through the back issues of February and March she noticed an article, followed by a letter, giving information about the Allen family. This housewife knew all about the Allen family and sent the following to the *Upton News*.

We lived in Tewkesbury and circumstances came about that we exchanged houses with an elderly couple named Allen who lived in Upton-on-Severn. On the Saturday before Christmas 1965 two friends of ours, a married couple, came over for the evening. The wife and I were eventually left on our own, my three children (aged ten months, three years, and four years nine months) having gone to bed and our husbands, who were both pigeon fanciers, having disappeared off to the pigeon club. At about 11 o'clock, I had just brought in some supper and we had started watching a good film when, quite suddenly, we heard children crying, followed by the sound of heavy footsteps as if several people were running from bedroom to bedroom across the landing. The strange thing was that it sounded as if they were running on bare boards and I had carpets all through. My friend said, 'That doesn't sound like your children'. I replied, 'It isn't!'. It's difficult to say how long it went on for, I should say about a minute, then the noise started coming down the stairs. At this point we both jumped up and rushed to the door which opened on to the hall, but as soon as we opened the door, the noise stopped and nothing was there. We went upstairs and all the children were fast asleep in bed. We couldn't understand what it was. We came downstairs and continued to watch the television. Half-an-hour later it happened a second time and again, as soon as I opened the door it stopped.

I went out to see if there was anything going on next door but the house was all in darkness, I heard later that they were out all evening. An elderly widow lived on the other side and I knew that she couldn't be responsible for the noise.

After Christmas the elderly widow asked me if I had had a nice Christmas. I answered, 'Yes, except for a strange noise' and I told her all about it. She said, 'That will be the Allen children'. She told me that there had been eleven children altogether in the family. Four of them had had diphtheria and were taken to the Upton-on-Severn Fever hospital. They were supposed to have been cured and all came home on the Friday evening but on the Saturday night the whole street was woken up by such a commotion. The children were screaming and the mother and father were in such a state, they were frantic. Eventually the neighbours managed to get hold of a doctor but he could do nothing and all four children died. An inquest was held but Mr Allen was not satisfied with the verdict. He insisted the Council remove the gas from the house and take up and relay the drains.

Some years later, Mrs Allen passed away and Mr Allen remarried, and the second Mrs Allen wanted to move from the house because of the haunting.

About eighteen months later, at the same time, I heard the strange noise again, and on that occasion I was in the house on my own. It was quite frightening. After a series of quite serious illnesses and bizarre accidents, plus the fact that we had to have the drains dug up when it was found that there were three fractures in the main sewers' pipe, we decided it was time for us to move.

One of the complications of diphtheria is cardiac arrest. A patient must lie perfectly still for several weeks after the illness, not even feeding him/herself. Would this have been possible with a large family, or would the excitement of returning home have been too much for them?

WORCESTERSHIRE VILLAGES

BLAKEDOWN

lakedown is known more for the roads that pass through it than for the village itself. In Roman times it was a saltway, running north from Droitwich, in 1777 the turnpike road from Kidderminster to Birmingham passed through it and now it is divided by both the A456 Kidderminster to Birmingham road and the B4188 to Belbroughton. It was on this latter road that Marie Skerratt had a surprise:

It happened about this time of the year (late October) somewhere between 1980 and 1985. I was going to a meeting and driving through Blakedown on the Belbroughton Road (B4188) . It was quiet and there was no other traffic behind me. Suddenly, I noticed a little old lady on the kerb, dithering and not knowing whether to cross or not. I stopped and let her go across the road. It was dusk and I thought, 'What is that little old lady doing out at this time of night all by herself?' She looked familiar to me so I studied her carefully. She was wearing a long skirt and she had an open-knit type shawl over head (perhaps crochet) and she was holding it at her neck. The shawl and the skirt were both black, but the shawl was a shade lighter than the skirt. Then I recognised her as old Mrs P. She was looking a bit agitated.

When she got to the other side she disappeared. As soon as she put her feet on the other side of the road she wasn't there any more. I knew she was a ghost immediately.

I got to this meeting and I said, 'I have seen a ghost'. They said, 'You don't look frightened'. Later, I said to the secretary of the meeting in Blakedown, 'I saw old Mrs P... crossing the road'. She said, 'You couldn't have done, she has been dead for four years'. When I described her she did agree that it sounded just like Mrs P.

My sister has moved from the village and is out of touch with things. I told her that I had seen this little old lady and described her, I didn't tell her that she had been a ghost. She said, 'Oh, that will be old Mrs P'. She didn't know that Mrs P had passed away.

I have not seen another ghost before or since.

BLISSGATE

Blissgate is a tiny village in an idyllic setting on the southern tip of the Wyre Forest in the district of Rock. This was once an important area, the local gentry, Henry de Ribbesford, had a grant of a weekly Wednesday market and an annual fair. Rock church is the largest Norman church in the county, beautifully ornate and well worth a visit. A young couple with a small child fell in love with the area and bought a house there in about 1989. The various unusual occurrences are told here by the wife's sister.

Their son is now ten and he was about two at the time so this must have occurred about eight years ago.

After they had lived in the house for some time, they had some work done on the house and when this started, my brother-in-law, Derek* and my sister both noticed a peculiar smell, like an unwashed person. Derek also often felt that someone was there. This feeling was so strong that he used to stand there and say, 'It's alright, we're only doing so-and-so' and he would describe out loud the work that was being done.

The main room was in the old part of the house, two stairs led out of this room, then there was a wooden door with one of the old-fashioned latches that you lift up, after which you came to a little landing and the remainder of the flight of stairs. One day, their small son was playing in this room and Derek was on the telephone to a relative, when the little boy suddenly began to chuckle and said, 'Daddy, man!'. He toddled over to his daddy and pointed to the door. Derek said to the relative, 'I'll talk to you later' and put the phone down. The boy said, 'Man, gone', pointed to the stairs door and pulled Derek through the doorway. They stood on the landing at the bottom of the stairs. The little boy looked up the stairs and started chuckling again. He started waving his arms to and fro, and saying, 'Man, tick tock'. Then he said, 'Oh, man gone!'

My brother-in-law and his wife are both convinced that their son saw something. It seems likely that he saw a man who had a watch on the chain and the man was swinging the watch to and fro.

They discovered that there had been an elderly gentleman living alone in the house at the beginning of the century.

BREDON HILL

This is one of Barrie Robert's gems. For most of the last thirty years Barrie has been a criminal lawyer but is now a full-time author. He has written five Sherlock Holmes novels and two Chris Tyroll mysteries.

South-west of Evesham, Bredon Hill stands nearly a thousand feet high above the Avon, surrounded by a circlet of pretty villages. Some of its slopes are rough and precipitous, but the hill is well worth climbing for the exceptional views.

Like most dramatic pieces of countryside, Bredon is capable of projecting an eerie atmosphere in certain lights and weathers, and at least one authority on the area believes that the Hill is haunted by a malevolent entity that could kill.

On the hill top are the ramparts of an iron Age fort, covering some eleven acres and containing an eighteenth century tower known as Parson's Folly. At some time a particularly vicious battle was fought there, for the remains of fifty victims have been found, savagely mutilated, with their heads, hands, feet and limbs hacked off and flung in a jumble.

Bredon Hill from Eckington bridge and the river Avon

Bredon Hill. The Bambury stone lies in the hollow to the left of Bredon Tower.

At one corner of the fort sits the Bambury Stone, which tradition asserts was a prehistoric sacrificial stone and later the focus of witchcraft activities. Harold T Wilkins, in 'Mysteries Solved and unsolved' derives the name 'Bambury' from 'ambrosie petrie' meaning 'anointed stone' and claims that the ancient stone was connected with the mysterious death of a local government clerk on Bredon Hill

At teatime on 9 May 1939, Harry Dean left his office and took a country bus to the village of Westmancote, below Bredon. From there he walked onto the Hill. Apparently, he and his wife intended to have a camping holiday somewhere on Bredon's slopes.

When Dean had not returned home by midnight the Police were called and a search began. At dawn Harry Dean's dead body was found, huddled at the foot of a boulder in an abandoned quarry.

At the inquest, Mrs Dean said that her husband was an athlete, playing county cricket, hockey and Rugby football. He had no enemies and no financial worries. He had had a slight injury to one leg that had weakened a cartilage, but it gave him no trouble.

A doctor told the inquest that Harry Dean had died of strangulation. She believed that he had climbed the boulder for a better view and had fallen, strangling himself with his own collar and tie. The Coroner agreed with her:

'I am convinced that Mr Dean did not fall more than three feet, and that he slipped, and displaced the cartilage of his leg. In great pain, he fainted, and was choked, owing to the unfortunate position in which he fell. It is a case of accidental death'.

No-one explained why he might have expected a better view from the top of the boulder. It was surrounded by the walls of the old quarry, from thirty to eighty feet high, and he could not have seen over them.

Harold T Wilkins visited the quarry, noting that the four curious, weathered boulders stood more or less at the cardinal points on the flat floor. Three were badly damaged but the fourth, on the south side, was where Dean was found.

From outside the quarry's entrance an ancient hollowed track, surrounded by prehistoric burial mounds, runs up the hill, passing two megaliths known as the King and Queen stones. Here, until about a century ago, villagers carried out an ancient practice of painting the stones white and passing around them the rheumatoid and the arthritic, in the believe that they would be relieved of their pain.

Wilkins described the path from the fatal quarry to the Bambury Stone, nearly a mile above it, and draws attention to the date of Dean's death - early May, a traditional time for ritual activity at prehistoric sites. He pours scorn, quite rightly, on the Coroner's peculiar verdict, and finally advances his own theory.

'He never climbed the boulder, in the 'Death Quarry', at whose base he was found strangled. he had no reason to do so, as one has already pointed out. In the dusk of that May night, in 1939, he may have approached the ring of pines on the edge of the northern rock wall of this quarry, and there, in the May darkness, something, some unpleasant entity, quite invisible, clutched his throat as he peered over the edge, and hurled him violently onto the floor of the quarry, some fifty or sixty feet below. Or, it may be that he entered the quarry, this ancient open air temple of paranoiac fertility rites, and was strangled by this unseen entity as he stood, in the dim light, at the base of that boulder.'

The strange death of poor Harry Dean will remain a mystery, but go to Bredon Hill and view the scene of the 'crime' and form your own opinions. Just don't go in the dusk - in early May!

BRETFORTON

About four miles east of Evesham is the cluster of picturesque houses known as Bretforton. Here is the Fleece Inn, owned by the National Trust, with the white lines still painted over the cracks on the floor to keep out the devil. In the parish church, on the top of one of the pillars there is a fascinating carving of Saint Margaret being swallowed by the devil. The saint was then supposed to have struck the devil with her cross so that his stomach split open and she was able to jump out.

The manor of Bretforton (ie the house and all its estates) once belonged to Evesham Abbey, which gave the profligate Abbot Roger Norreys (see Evesham) an excuse to come here once a year and hold a great feast. It was reported that he 'squandered the rentals of the sacrist in luxury and drunkenness, spending on one day what would have sufficed the members of the church for a year'.

The old Bretforton Manor, a three-bay stone house with three gables dated 1605, still stands near to the church. A lady who once lived in Bretforton but now lives in Hampton, tells the story:

Bretforton - where a long-gone Lady of the Manor walks the road outside.

Just after the war, sometime in the 1950's, my mother used to go folk dancing. She was with a group of young ladies who were returning home about nine o'clock one night and they were walking down the street between the manor and a big house on the left when this white female ghost walked past. One of the ladies said, 'Good evening' and there was no answer. Again she said, 'Good evening' and still there was no answer so she replied 'Blast you then!'. They used to say that a lady who once lived at the manor used to walk the road outside.

When Gemma Taylor* was working as an auxiliary nurse at Avonside, one of the SRNs moved to a house in Bretforton and each night ...

In those days, you had to go to the office to collect your salary. I happened to bump into her there one day and she was as white as a sheet. She said, 'Don't talk to me, I'm in a bad temper' and I said, 'I hope you feel better tonight because I'm working with you'. She answered, 'Oh, I'm sorry, it's just that something has happened!'

That night I sat opposite her and I said, 'Well, are you going to tell me or aren't you?' and she replied, 'Only if you swear not to tell a soul'. Thinking she was going to tell me about some family matter I agreed and to my surprise she said, 'I've seen a ghost!'

Evidently she was taking the dog for a walk and just as she was coming up to a bend in the road she saw an old lady with a basket over her arm crossing the road. She was so slow that my friend said to herself (using her exact words) 'Hurry up, you silly old b.... or you'll get knocked over'. When the old lady reached the other side of the road she disappeared through the wall. The dog started yelping and his hairs stood on end, the hairs on the back of her neck stood up too.

If you call into the local pub at Bretforton many of the regulars there have seen the old lady crossing the road and they say that she is carrying a basket of eggs.

A visit to the Victoria Arms (which is now closed) and the Fleece only resulted in tales of the ghost of Lola Taplin, which were published in 'Haunted Pubs and Hotels'.

BROADWAY

Broadway advertises its location by means of Broadway Tower, with its three round turrets topped by battlements. It was built as a folly by the Earl of Coventry in 1798 at his wife's whim. On a clear day it can be seen from thirteen counties - but not from Broadway itself.

The village of Broadway is at least 1,000 years old and is built almost entirely of mellowed Cotswold stone. Pevsner describes it as 'the show village of England'. It has a Hotel going back to 1532 and a Norman church with a gatehouse where both Charles I and Oliver Cromwell stayed (not at the same time).

During summer weekends the village is crowded with tourists and with so many people and such an ancient history the village has many tales of ghosts. One of the legends concerns a lady who was killed while hunting and her ghost has been seen innumerable times in White Ladies Lane, a deep gully at the top end of the village.

A local housekeeper has another tale to tell.

When they have a party on the Broadway, it is some party. They even have mattresses laid out in the hall for those who can't make it up the stairs.

I think the year was 1987 when I was housekeeper of a very old three-storied house in a little village near the Broadway. It was the day after Boxing Day, the snow was deep and the owners had just left after a party. I was on my own and the house was an absolute wreck. I started at 7.15 in the morning and I thought, 'First, I'll get the bed linen tagged and put them in the book for the laundry lady to collect, that will be a help. Then I looked out of the window and saw that a little red car was parked outside. That meant that one of the family's guests was still sleeping upstairs so that I couldn't go up.

At ten o'clock I decided I would have to go upstairs. Now, on the middle floor was what was known as 'The White Room', a beautiful room decorated in white from floor to ceiling. As I went to the door I felt that someone was in there so I thought, 'Maybe I'll give it a bit longer'. So I went to the other bedrooms and did that laundry. Suddenly, I heard the red car driving off, it must have belonged to the farmer next door who wasn't supposed to park on our property. I thought, 'Who the deuce is in that room? Well, I'll have to go in there and if someone is there I'll just have to plead ignorance'.

I'm not a fanciful person at all, my life has been much too hard for that, but as I got to the door I felt intimidated. I said to myself, 'This is ridiculous, there is nobody there'. I knocked the door before I opened it then I nearly jumped against the wall. Something sailed past me, like an invisible block, as if someone was there taking over my will. As it went past I picked up that it was a very small lady in a crinoline-type dress. She was so very gentle and so very lovely I followed her downstairs and then she disappeared. It's difficult to explain the feeling but it was quite real. I can only describe it by saying that you know when you are in a room and someone you love comes in, even thought you don't look at them you are aware of them - it's as if you have honed in on them. It's like a chemical reaction or as if you have tuned into their wavelength.

Anyway, it was obvious that I wasn't going to get all the work done so I rang up my bosses' secretary who looked after everything and asked her if I could have some help. Then I said to her, 'By the way, I have just had a most uncanny experience'. She said, 'Oh, you're not going to leave are you? The last woman we had rushed out in a panic because she said she had seen the ghost of a little old lady. She said that this lady was very small and she had a big dress on'.

CAUNSALL

Caunsall is a tiny hamlet on the river Stour, just under a mile from Stourbridge and just over a mile from Wolverley. Historians know that there was a thriving monastery at Wolverley but Ron Griffin thinks that there was also one at Caunsall.

I live in an old cottage, just below the canal bridge and a little to the left of an iron bridge over the river Stour. The meadow leads to Caunsall where I used to visit friends at Caunsall House farm. According to a local historian, the late Mr Beaston, Caunsall House Farm was on the site of a monastery.

It was often a little scary coming back across the meadow. One night I was just crossing the iron bridge when I saw a dark figure on the canal bridge. I quickened my footsteps to catch the man up as I thought it might be company.

I reached within a few steps of him and saw that the man appeared to be wearing a duffle coat and hood. He strode on in front of me, yet I heard no sound of footsteps. I kept quiet, for fear of disturbing him. When we reached the summit of the bank, I could see the dark figure plainly against the night sky. He then suddenly vanished in front of me. Realising it was not a human being, I fled down to the cottage and couldn't get inside quick enough.

Could it have been one of the monks accompanying me back to my cottage?

CLENT

A thousand years ago Clent was a place of great importance. It was the King's land, and early historians speak of a royal palace on the north-eastern slope of the hill. It could have been the residence of the great Mercian king, Offa, who built Offa's Dyke before he died in about 794. After Kenulph's death it is said that Kenelm, the eight-year old boy, became king. His murder, and the appearance of a spring where his body was found, near St Kenelm's church, is described in *Haunted Worcestershire*.

Another curious tale comes from Margaret, who lives in the village.

Our house used to be occupied by an elderly couple and their daughter. The father died, then the mother, and the daughter decided to move down south. We bought the house from her.

At the top of the stairs was a short corridor and whenever we went on this landing both my husband and I had this strange feeling that someone else was there. A few months after we had moved, we had this knock on the door and there was the daughter. She said, 'I've come to collect my mum!'. She told us that she used to feel her mum was still in the

St Kenelm's church at Clent

house and the mother hadn't moved with her to her new house. We told her about this strange feeling we had and she said, 'Oh yes, that's my mum'. Evidently, when her mother was alive she used to keep going across the landing from her bedroom to her father's bedroom to make sure he was alright as he was often ill.

Whether the daughter managed to collect her mother or not, I don't know, all that I can say is that the feeling disappeared from the landing.

CUTNALL GREEN

Cutnall Green is about three miles north of Droitwich. This is an area rich in ghosts and legends. To the north is Harvington Hall, to the west is Hartlebury Castle and Bromsgrove is to the east. About a mile to the north is Rushock Court, where tradition says a Roman Catholic priest was beheaded in the time of the religious persecutions. His head rolled down Church Hill and came to a halt in a hedge. Since then nothing will grow there.

The next narrator is well-known in the area and an official of more than one voluntary society.

This is an early Georgian house about 200 years old. It has always been a farmhouse and at one time it was joined to the barns which are about 400 years old. We have taken the house apart and totally rebuilt it.

The following incident happened about four years ago on one of my sleepless nights. I was sitting up in bed with my head against the headboard when this tall, dark figure came from behind my bed, that is, from the old part of the house which has now been made into a bathroom, walked alongside my bed, round the foot and out though the doorway. I could just see the silhouette of a very tall lady with a long grey gown of the type worn in the Scottish Widows' advertisement. She was walking very slowly but I would guess that she was quite young. It wasn't so much that I could see her but I knew without a doubt that she was there.

The stairway from our bedroom led to the nanny's quarters so my wife and I have decided that it must have been a nanny that I saw.

That is the only one time that I have seen anything out of the ordinary. Nothing else peculiar has happened in all the years that we have been here.

EARL'S CROOME AND RYALL

Ryall is one of those places that many people know of but few have visited, the reason being that the junction of the M5 and M50 is signposted Ryall. It lies between the A38 and the River Severn, with a large marina on its western edge. About a mile from Ryall is Earl's Croome, originally called 'Crumba!' but the 'Earl' was added when the it came under the patronage of the Earl of Warwick in 1369.

The village has a traditional ghost crossing the A38 but the mother and son who saw it in 1976 did not know about the legend at that time.

We came to live in Earls Croome in 1970. One winter evening in 1976 I went to collect my fourteen-year old son from his friend's house in Ryall. The return journey took us up the A38 towards the Yorkshire Grey. It was about 10.15 on a clear, calm night. As we approached the entrance drive to Levant Lodge, a figure suddenly appeared in the middle of the road. I slammed on the brakes so hard that I stalled the car. The figure glided in front of us, across the verge and straight through the hedge, which was higher then, into Levant Lodge grounds.

I said to my son, 'Did you see that?'. He said it looked like someone hunched up in a long brown overcoat but it didn't seem to have any feet. I thought it was a long brown riding Mac with the collar turned up, and wearing a brimmed hat. The stance was of someone walking against driving rain or gale force wind. I did not see any feet.

I started the car and eased it forward. My son opened the door and looked out. He confirmed that whatever it was had gone straight through the hedge and we both decided we had seen a ghost.

HAGLEY

The parish of Hagley was at one time part of the Forest of Kinver but it became common land in about 1300. The main roads from Stourbridge to Bromsgrove and from Kidderminster to Halesowen passed through the parish.

Hagley Hall was built between 1754 and 1760 for the first Lord Lyttleton. It was based on the classical style, with the use of columns and other details found in ancient Greek and Roman remains. Everything was order and regularity. Pevsner describes it as Palladio-Inigo-Jones. It was fashionable to make miniature copies of various buildings in Athens, which were carefully measured up, and place them in the grounds of stately homes. Hagley is exceptionally rich in these, among them The Temple of Theseus on the main road to Birmingham. The interior was seriously damaged by a fire in 1925 but restored in 1926.

There had been a hall on the site before then, built mainly of wood. It was in this old hall that Robert Wintour and Stephen Lyttleton, two of the conspirators of the Gunpowder Plot were captured. They had escaped from Holbeach House and, not knowing where to go, decided to risk a visit to the Lyttleton residence. A man called Peck concealed them in his house, then during the absence of Mrs Lyttleton, took them to the hall but they were betrayed by one of the servants.

Lord Lyttleton also owned Pitt Place, in Epsom, Surrey. While his son, the second Lord Lyttleton, was staying there in November 1779 he was warned that he only had three days to live. The story varies; in some versions he was warned by a ghost, in others by an angel while yet other versions state that

Hagley Hall

111

it was the fluttering of a bird at the window. The last seems the most likely, especially as this was thought to be a sign of impending death and Lord Lyttleton was very superstitious. He seemed perfectly healthy until the final hour of the three days when he suddenly died from 'a seizure'.

The second Lord Lyttleton often went to stay with a friend, Miles Andrews, who lived at Dartford in Kent. Somewhere near midnight of that third day Miles awoke to see Lyttleton in his bedroom, wearing the dressing gown that was kept for his use when he came to stay. Lyttleton said, 'It's all up with me, Andrews' and walked into the dressing room. Miles followed him into the dressing room and was surprised to find it empty and the dressing gown hanging on a hook. He thought that, in some way, Lyttleton was playing a trick on him and he returned to his bed. In the morning he learned that Lord Lyttleton had passed away.

In reply to an enquiry if there were any recent hauntings at Hagley Hall, Lord Cobham's personal assistant wrote:

> I asked him about any ghost stories etc, and it seems that a spinet has been heard to play in the Long Gallery on the occasions when the house is "jolly and full". Lord Cobham's younger brother, The Hon Richard Lyttelton was once playing the piano in the Crimson Drawing Room whilst the family were sitting in the Library. He rushed in with his hair 'standing on end' as he had heard the spinet joining in with his playing! The spinet has also been heard by Penelope, Viscountess Cobham who was Lord Cobham's former wife.

The angel appears to Lord Lyttleton. (The Astrologer, 1825)

HANBURY

Hanbury is scattered across two miles of some of the loveliest countryside in England, with deep winding lanes, huge trees and gentle hills. It is thought that the name is Saxon and means 'High Town'. The B4090, which runs from Droitwich through Feckenham, is an old Roman road and a saltway. It passes through Hanbury, then, going towards Feckenham, it climbs a hill. At the top of this hill is a large house currently occupied by Ceramaspeed Ltd. This is Hadzor Hall which, according to local historians, stands on the site of an ancient monastery. There is an old village tradition, handed down from generation to generation, that a monk committed suicide on top of the hill but before he did so, he cursed the area from Pack Hill to Hallowfield. Over the past few centuries this area has had more than its fair share of road accidents and family tragedies, and many an inhabitant of Hanbury attributes them to the monk's curse.

One of these tragedies occurred during the last world war. Although he was only a small child at the time, Robin Cook can clearly remember the plane crash. The plane was on fire when it flew over his house, the engine dropped off and landed in a pool and the passengers ejected but their parachutes caught fire. It occurred before Alan Thomas was born but he heard about it from his parents:

> My parents lived in one of the farm worker's cottages on a farm at Hanbury. The cottages are still there, to the east of the Jinney Ring Craft Centre. Towards the end of the last world war or just after it, a Lancaster bomber crashed on to Platt's fields nearby, not far from the Deer Pans. My dad rushed out to see if he could help but there was nothing he could do. One of the airmen was hanging in a tree, obviously dead, and the plane was burning so vigorously, with ammunition exploding, that he couldn't get anywhere near it. He did take away a couple of souvenirs which he later gave away.
>
> All those aboard the plane were killed. There were eight of them, all Canadians, one of them was a passenger who shouldn't have been on the plane at all.
>
> Many years later, when I was about sixteen, I had a friend of the same age who took a short cut across those fields late one evening and saw a grey figure hovering in the field. He was terrified. He shook as he told me about it. At that time, neither of us had heard about the bomber, so I assumed that what he had seen was a scarecrow and told him so, but he was adamant that he had seen a ghost.

Robin Cook, a local historian, says that the number of planes that crashed in this area is surprising. There was an aerodrome at Honeybourne and another at Pershore, so the planes would limp home and not manage the last lap.

Hanbury is dominated by two buildings. The one is the old church, standing high on the hill, the other is Hanbury Hall, which was built by Thomas Vernon in about 1700.

The story of his great grand-daughter, Emma Vernon, who was married to a member of the Cecil family but absconded with the local curate, is given

Hadzor Hall and church, between Droitwich and Hanbury, said to be built on the site of an old monastery

in *Haunted Worcestershire*. Since that time innumerable people have seen the ghost of Emma Vernon. Traditionally, the ghost walks from the church to some old stables a short way down the hill but the locals reckon that she has been seen all round the area. Mary Fletcher lives about a mile away, opposite the 'Country Girl'.

In the early 1970's I was taking my dog for a walk one autumn morning at about 11 o'clock. Then as I came up the path leading towards the church, I caught sight of a black figure wearing a cloak disappearing round the far corner of the church. I thought, Oh, there's someone in the churchyard. I looked all round the churchyard and in the car park, but there was no-one to be seen and the car park was empty. I had heard all the local stories about Emma Vernon but had pooh-poohed them. I was quite shattered.

Katie is a Solicitor's Assistant:

I like going out to country areas and I'd heard about Hanbury. I'd read bits and pieces and I'd picked some things up from other people so I went with a friend to have a look round in the early spring of about 1988. We were walking round the north side of the church when I saw the figure of a woman by the side of me. I looked again and she had gone. I thought, 'Something's not quite right here'. It was a very fleeting experience. I felt that she was not of our age but was someone who had come and gone. I didn't say anything to my friend, I felt rather embarrassed. Afterwards I mentioned it to one or two people.

I'm not really sure what I saw. It was something I happened to witness, I just quickly noticed someone. I don't want to make too much of it really.

The next incident concerns one of those inexplicable roadside apparitions, seen here by Dudley Fowkes. Dudley is a semi-retired teacher/musician and of all the professions, that of teacher must produce an individual who has an analytical and sceptical approach to events, yet he was terrified by something on that country road. It's obviously not Emma Vernon and there is no particular reason why a participant of the Civil War should appear in this area.

This happened one Saturday evening about February/March time in the early 1970's, either just before or just after midnight. I had been playing percussion at a Symphony Concert performed at the Worcester Teacher Training College and was returning to my home in Crabbs Cross (just outside Redditch) in my new Vauxhall Victor Estate, of which I was very proud. When I reached Droitwich I decided to finish my journey along the country lane which runs from the Jinney Ring Craft Centre at Hanbury to the Bramley Cottage on Windmill Drive.

I was on the straight road on the far side of Elcocks Brook, not going very quickly because it was misty and I was tired, when I saw this figure on the left hand side of the road. I can see him in my mind's eye now. He was of average build and wearing what appeared to be a long dark-coloured cloak and a wide-brimmed floppy hat of the type worn in the Roundheads and Cavaliers era. I thought, 'Who the devil is that walking alone, at midnight, miles away from anywhere?'. I slowed down as I went past him (I think it was a 'he', I have no reason to believe it was a 'her') but I didn't see his face as I was looking at the road.

A bit further on I looked in my rear mirror and couldn't see the figure, so, thinking somebody might need a lift as there were no houses for a mile or so, I stopped, opened the door and got out. I stood listening but I couldn't hear a sound, no rustling, no footsteps, nothing. I decided to wait and see if the figure wanted a lift. I waited one or two minutes or perhaps five minutes. When I thought I had waited sufficient time for the person to have reached me - and when the figure never came - I jumped in the car and drove home. I was frightened to death; I woke my wife up to tell her about it and she said later that I had looked terrified.

I visit Hanbury Hall quite frequently but I have not since seen that figure, perhaps because I now don't return when it's dark, and never when it's approaching midnight.

INKBERROW

Despite the march of progress Inkberrow still has its village green, still surrounded by brick and timber-framed buildings. One of these is the Old Bull, the inspiration for 'The Archers', another is the Vicarage, where Charles I stayed on his way to the battle of Naseby and left his maps behind. In retaliation, the Parliamentarians desecrated parts of the church, chopping the legs off one of the monuments.

There are several haunted houses in Inkberrow and here, the residents tend to be rather fond of their ghosts. Micky* is one of them.

As soon as I walked into the house which was for sale in Inkberrow I decided that I had to buy it. I felt enfolded in the house's friendliness, The deeds went back to the eighteenth century but the house had been built before then and had once been two or three workmen's cottages. The front half was thatched but the back of the house had suffered a fire and had a tiled roof.

We moved from a long way away and so we had no chance to visit the house again before we actually moved, in the usual chaos and fury. We did not get to bed until midnight and, completely exhausted, we slept deeply. In the morning, my wife asked why I had left the kitchen door open. I felt sure I had fastened the door, but being very tired, might not have done so. However, every night afterwards, I shut the door most carefully and every morning it was open.

Eventually, we just accepted it as we did the many other strange occurrences. Why was there a ring of wet sherry on the dresser one morning? There was no sherry in the house, nor had there been for some weeks. Who moved my gun from inside its cupboard to behind the front door? Cases and clothes were often moved, but always neatly, nothing was ever thrown about. Sometimes a cloud drifted across the little sitting room to disappear through the wall. The dogs used to sit up, watch it pass, then lie down again.

Something strange or unusual happened to every guest, but nothing frightening ever occurred and the same thing never happened twice. My brother and his wife awoke in the early hours to see the vacuum cleaner silently Hoovering away. My cousin, Paul, worked at Smithfield market and was therefore an early riser. He set his alarm for four o'clock in the morning and was annoyed when it went off at one. It had never misbehaved before. Thinking he'd made a mistake, he reset it for four again and it went off at two. Very carefully, this time he reset it once more for four, saying aloud, "If that's Micky's ghost messing about with my clock, if you do it again, I'll go!" The clock went off at three so he got up and departed.

I tried to find out more about the history of the house but no-one seemed to know much about it. We asked our predecessors if they had thought the house was haunted, but they had had several children and I don't think they would have noticed if the house had been moved overnight! I happened to meet the local Fire Chief and asked him about the fire which had destroyed half the house. He told me that it was one of the most extraordinary fires he had ever attended. The fire station was six miles away from the house, along winding country roads, and as wattle and daub houses burn very quickly they expected to find a smouldering ruin when they arrived, but not a bit of it - the fire had stopped exactly halfway across the thatch and only a few of the timbers underneath were charred.

We loved the house - I was often away on business trips for a few days but I had no qualms at leaving my wife alone. She always said, "The house will look after me!". However, it proved too expensive to run so that when a smaller house nearby became available we purchased that one and put ours on the market. The first people to see the house fell in love with it and bought it.

Shortly afterwards the new owner invited my wife round to see a new window inserted in the little sitting room. "Very nice", said my wife, "But why did you have it put in?". "Oh well" replied the occupant, "The wall fell down and the builder said it wasn't strong enough to build up, so we put in another window. The ghost loves it!". We never found out how she knew, and I have never dared to ask.

LITTLE COMBERTON

Nestling at the foot of Bredon Hill is the tiny village of Little Comberton, with its twelfth century church and half-timbered houses. However, it's not in the medieval homes that the manifestation appears, but in a modern bungalow, currently inhabited by Maurice Nelson.

> We have lived here for just over six years. During the last three years my wife has got this smell of cigarette smoke. I can't smell it at all. For example, we're in the kitchen and my wife says, 'Can't you smell it?' Then she says, 'You come over here, to where I'm standing, and you're sure to smell it', and I go over there but I can't smell it.
>
> She has made such a fuss about it that I have had all the boards up just in case something is smouldering underneath, but there's nothing. My sense of smell is just as good as hers, if not better, and so if something was on fire I should be able to smell it as well.
>
> For the last week she has been woken up in the night by what feels like someone blowing a puff of smoke over her face. Over the last few days, as well, the fire alarm has been pinging for about two hours every night. It was such a nuisance I have taken the battery out and I have just put a new one in. However, I don't think it's the battery because it would ping all the time instead of just in the night.
>
> We found out that someone who had the bungalow before us, not the last person but the one before, was a tobacconist. He passed away some years ago.

LITTLE HEREFORD

As you drive along the A456 from Tenbury Wells to Woofferton, watch out for the tiny track which leads to Little Hereford Church. The tower is thirteenth century with a pyramid roof and inside the church is one of the best-preserved set of rood stairs in the county. In the meadow beyond the churchyard are interesting-looking bumps and ridges which feature in the next incident, told by Terry Hill, a member of the local historical society:

> Some of the members of the Tenbury Wells and District Civic and Historical Society had done some research on a site in Little Hereford, at the back of the fortified church. I think it was in 1993 that we were asked by the Worcestershire Archaeological Society to lay on an open day. Three or four of us went from the Society - Howard Miller, John Asquith and myself - and we took some ladies whom we intended to train to act as guides on the day. It was a very hot summer evening in August and we were all in our shirt sleeves. The site is little more than a series of platforms, we were walking along these and I was showing them where everything had been, when one of the ladies suddenly

Little Hereford Church

clutched my arm so fiercely that her nails bit into my skin and the hair on her arms stood up on end. She cried, 'Please get me away from this terrible place'. She was in a dreadful state. She said that she could see the roofs of thatched cottages on fire and women and children being mutilated and butchered. Her husband was in another group so we called him over and he said, 'Oh yes, she's psychic'. She was so upset that she has since left the society.

When she described the scene she mentioned two towers, one each side of the site. The following day we scratched about in the soil and we found the remains of a circular tower on the one side. The other side is now under the river but there was a lot of dressed stone in the bank which suggests that a building of some kind was there.

We looked into the history of the site and found that the Welsh raided the area several times. A G Bradley, in his book *In the March and Borderland of Wales* (published in 1905 by Constable) writes that they had once caught the people before they could get into the church. They put the village to the torch, butchered the children and raped the women. Also, according to Thomas Habington, the Elizabethan historian, the Danes are known to have "ravenously sacked" this area.

Little Hereford Church

MARTLEY AND WICHENFORD

About four miles north-west of Worcester is the privately-owned Wichenford Court. It was once the home of the Washbourne family, when it was one of the largest mansions in the county, and had a moat and drawbridge. Much of the present building dates back to 1712. Although the Court is privately-owned, the well-preserved dovecote is open to the public.

Wichenford has had a sinister reputation. When the Worcester Naturalists Club visited the Court in 1866, they reported that around two sides of an oak-panelled room were numbers of carved, grinning heads, filled with human teeth.

According to the *Victoria County History*, during the reign of Henry IV (1399-1413), a member of the French aristocracy was held prisoner at Wichenford Court. This may be true because at that time, the English were fighting the Welsh (led by Owen Glendower) and the French had sent troops to help the Welsh. The then Lady Washbourne stabbed the Frenchman to death. A local story is that she fell in love with her prisoner and murdered him when he rejected her advances. After her death her ghost was seen in the murdered noble's bedchamber, dagger in hand.

One of the Lords of the Manor of Wichenford was executed in 1553. This was John Dudley, Duke of Northumberland.

A later member of the Washbourne family was an ardent Royalist and probably fought for Charles in the battle of Worcester in 1651. His wife is said to haunt the moat holding a golden harp in a silver boat drawn by four white swans.

Just over a mile to the west is the ancient and beautifully-preserved village of Martley. The church is chiefly twelfth century. Below the church is St Paul's well, which is older still, and probably used for baptisms before the church was built.

The half-timbered home of the Wood* family overlooks the centre of the village. There are four family members, the parents and two children, David

and Emily, both in their early twenties. This particular evening, the velvet curtains are drawn across the French windows and as the flames of the log fire flicker on the low ceilings, they each take it in turns to tell their story:

David:

The poltergeist was a terrible nuisance. We used to get up in the morning and find all the electrics on, the lights and my computer would be on and the television and radio would be blaring away. Everyone used to blame me. Sometimes I would come home to find a picture smashed, and once I found a knife and fork crossed in the middle of the floor. It got past a joke; it was quite worrying.

In 1991, I had a friend staying over and he slept on the floor of my bedroom. I fell asleep but my friend lay awake. Later, he said he was convinced that he saw a dark figure sitting on the end of my bed, sideways on, looking at the wall. He reached up and tried to shake me awake but I wouldn't wake up, my friend said I seemed to be comatosed. He jumped out of bed and switched the light on. The dark figure disappeared but something smacked his leg. The next morning he complained to the rest of the family and when he showed us his leg, we saw that there were finger bruises on it. While we were talking about it there was a loud crash overhead, the family rushed upstairs but we have never found out what caused it.

Emily:

The poltergeist didn't seem to bother me as much as the others, which was strange because it was obvious that it didn't like me and was trying to get rid of me. I was fifteen when we first moved here and there were the usual framed school photographs around the living room. Quite often, we used to come home to find one of them smashed on the floor. We would get it reframed, then it would smash again. There was a picture of me under the magnet on the fridge and suddenly, while I was in the kitchen, the photograph removed itself from under the magnet and flew over to the other side of the room.

It was usually my possessions that went missing, I know that sometimes I do put things in the wrong place but articles turned up in the most weird places. For example, I keep my scissors in a red tin and they turned up in a pot on the shelf. I would never put them there! We still get the occasional event, about six months ago I was lying in my bed and the quilt was going up and down all by itself, but it never bothers me.

Mrs Wood:

We have had problems in some of the other older houses that we have lived in but they were only minor such as footsteps and rattling door handles. Nothing, anywhere else was as bad as this.

The house was full of noises, you expect it with an old house but several times I have heard footsteps and thought my husband was out of bed and when I went upstairs he was fast asleep.

About once a week we would hear the sound of something falling over with such force that it smashed. We would go and have a look but nothing had ever moved. We still have the occasional crash but we ignore it now and don't bother. Normally, we're all working and out all day, but I decided to come home one lunch time and I was greeted by a river of water rushing down the stairs. All the taps had been turned full on. Everything was drenched.

This poltergeist has been a terrible experience, above all it affected your mood. You came in quite cheerful and after a few minutes, you felt as if life wasn't worth living. The only way I could face living here was by spending the evening in an alcoholic haze. I'm afraid I took to drink.

My husband was totally changed - he wasn't the same person, he was just awful. He would explode at the slightest thing. In the end he left home. The night that he moved out two photographs, one of Emily and one of David, flew from off the top of the telly to the other side of the room and smashed at my feet. I couldn't believe it. I had a look to see if they were on springs or anything but the frame was solid brass.

Mr Wood

When we moved in we discovered that we had a poltergeist. Its activities were a nuisance but I could cope with that. What I couldn't cope with was the terrible depression that seemed to come with it. Over the next couple of years it got worse and worse. In the end, I just couldn't stop in the house any longer. I just felt that I had to leave so I packed my bags and went to stay with my mother.

In the end I said that enough was enough and, we decided to get the house exorcised in March 1990. A spiritualist arrived one Sunday evening. He knelt down, holding a cross, and he seemed to go into a trance. All of a sudden, this terrible whirlwind filled the house, it felt as if the room was spinning and then all went quiet. The room turned icy cold. The medium was shaking, he said that it had been a struggle and the entity didn't want to leave.

Since we had the house exorcised things have quietened down but we still get the odd event from time to time. Last week the curtains across the French windows were moving right out as if they were being blown by a gale but there was no draught and no wind. The windows were rattling violently as if someone was trying to get in. My wife opened and closed them a few times and then they stopped. That was in the daylight, not at night.

It is fairly common knowledge that hauntings of the noisy poltergeist type frequently seem to revolve around pubescent children, usually female and often either ill or under some kind of stress. It is not unknown for poltergeist activity to be linked to a personality change, although this is usually of the person creating the activity.

Barrie Roberts comments:

They do, certainly, attack photographs, usually of people against whom there is repressed hostility. As to 'exorcism', this is an ancient ritual of the Catholic and Anglican churches, never carried out without the permission of a bishop. It is specifically intended to drive out evil spirits. Since poltergeists are not evil spirits, but manifestations of hostility and stress by someone within the household, exorcism will not get rid of them and may make them worse. Eight hundred years ago Giraldus Cambrensis, who was a senior cleric himself, wrote the first account of British poltergeists in 'A Journey Through Wales'. He also recorded that the efforts of ordained priests to exorcise them had been unsuccessful and that the priests had had filth and verbal abuse flung at them.

SALFORD HALL

Rob Ward has been looking through his family archives and has discovered information about the hall which should go down on record. Salford Hall was the home of Robert Stanford who left the hall first, to his wife, then to certain members of the Berkeley family, then to the Eyston family. The widow of Robert Stanford allowed the English Benedictine Dames of Cambria (who had fled from the French Revolution in 1808) to have Salford Hall rent-free for her lifetime and Robert Berkeley consented, at her request, to let them stay during his life-time also. But obviously they had to find somewhere permanent to live, and so, in 1838, they went to Stanbrook Abbey. Captain Eyston sold the hall to a Mr Hughes who was more interested in the land, so he sold off all the beautiful furniture and much damage was done to the hall. Rob Ward continues:

When a relative of mine, Kath Bridges, was first married, she and her husband, Wilf, lived with her mother whom we called 'Aunt Nell'. Aunt Nell was housekeeper and custodian for the Roman Catholic priests of Salford Hall. That was in the late 1920's or early 1930's, and in those days it was called, 'The Nunnery'.

One day I said to her, 'I've heard that Salford Hall is haunted, is that correct?' and she replied, 'It certainly is'. She told me that one night, she and her husband were in bed when they saw a tall shadow standing at the foot of the bed. It stayed there without moving, then gradually faded away. Another night, they were both in bed when the bed levitated two or three feet off the floor before it gently settled back down. They never slept in that room again.

Tales of a ghostly priest and two little American girls were featured in 'Haunted Pubs and Hotels'.

Salford Hall, now restored and converted into an hotel.

SEVERN STOKE

Two miles north of Upton-on-Severn, on the A38, is the village of Severn Stoke. It is said that there are more apparitions here than houses. A Roman solider is said to walk round Knightshill pool, holding his head under his arm. A Roman cavalry rides through the village, inhabitants can hear the clink of their armour. And people have heard footsteps in the local folly, when no-one is there. The village comprises little more than a church with Norman fragments, a few houses and a large fourteenth century, half-timbered building. Although this is now a restaurant, it is still known as the Old School House.

During the 1970's and 1980's it was converted into a country club. Serena Chancellor's mother worked there and sometimes Serena would accompany her.

I was playing there one day when I was about eight years old and I had this strange sensation. There was a top bar and a bottom bar, both on the same level but the top bar was the one nearest the house. I turned towards the top bar, where it's very dark, and I saw a shadow moving, Although it was dark in that area, the shadow was a solid black silhouette, darker than room. I could see that it had a flat hat with a tassle hanging from it, it looked like a mortar board. One arm was outstretched as it glided towards the hall and straight through the wall. I noticed that the room went very cold.

When I left school in 1987, I went to the Country Club as an Assistant Cook. I was working late at eleven o'clock one night when I heard footsteps going across the old dance floor above me. I went upstairs to see if anybody had sneaked in when my back was turned. I could hear these heavy footsteps slowly and steadily advancing towards me but nobody was there.

I was often working late and most of the times that I was there at eleven o'clock I would hear them. My older brother was a DJ there and my younger brother often helped him. They both heard the footsteps. Usually the footsteps went across the dance floor, down the stairs and round and round the building. They would go on for an hour or two.

Other things would happen. Doors would slam, lights would come on of their own accord and the next morning we would see that things had been moved, for example, the pictures would be all skewiff.

It is said that the old schoolmaster hanged himself on the top floor.

STOKE PRIOR

Elms Farm

The world-famous composer, Sir Edward Elgar, was very much a Worcestershire man. He was born at Broadheath in 1857 and gained most of his musical knowledge and experience from his work with local musical societies. His first success was the production of King Olaf at Hanley in 1893. He often composed while walking the Malvern hills.

By 1900 he had achieved a national reputation with the Enigma Variations, Sea Pictures and The Dream of Gerontius.

Elms Farm is a house which Elgar loved. He composed some of his music here, in a large, light room at the end of the house, overlooking green fields and away from the general household noise. He bought Elms Farm for his sister Dorothy of whom he was extremely fond. When he heard that he was to be knighted his first reaction was to jump on his bike and ride over to tell Dorothy. Rumour has it that he and his wife were not happily married and after each disagreement Elgar would go round to his sister's to be fed and looked after.

Ask the present owner, Peter Loftus, how old this lovely, half-timbered farm is and he replies that the new bits are 1635. When he bought it in 1985 most of the timbers were rotten to floor level and had to be replaced. Peter managed to find old plans and is restoring the house to pre-Victorian layout. His work has been commended by the Bromsgrove Society.

The size of the house and the carved beams in the kitchen show that it originally belonged to someone of some status. The converted bathroom alone is almost the size of a small classroom and it was here that Peter first experienced a strange visitor.

> I was repanelling a wall and sawing wood at an angle so I was concentrating very hard. Then someone came into the room and said something. I can't remember what it was, it may have been, 'What are you doing here?' or something like that. When I finished sawing and looked up, no-one was there. I was so certain that someone had spoken to me that I shouted to my wife, 'Did you say something to me then?' but she hadn't. This has happened to us all so often - to my wife, to my cleaner, to all sorts of people, time and time again.
>
> My daughter was the first one to notice something strange when she was about two. She said, 'What was that orange light in the doorway of my bedroom last night?'. We investigated carefully but could find nothing to explain it.
>
> It always seems to appear when you are engrossed in something. To describe it I would say, imagine that you are speaking to someone on the telephone and trying to read something in front of you at the same time, then somebody comes in through the door and speaks to you. You know that someone has appeared and you know that someone has said something but you don't know exactly what.
>
> I'm sure that whatever-it-is, is quite benevolent. There is nothing sinister about the house at all, it has a warm, happy feeling.

STUDLEY

Studley lies just outside the Worcestershire/Warwickshire border on the old Roman Icknield Street, the A435. Despite the ultra-modern supermarket in the centre, which locals are surprised to learn has won various design awards, this is an ancient village. Studley church has a small Norman doorway and there was an old castle which has now completely disappeared. The village has moved over the centuries so that whereas it once lay on the western side of the A435 it now lies on the eastern side and the old church is surrounded by farmland.

The prize-winning Jubilee public house is on the A448, halfway between Crabbs Cross island and the old Roman road, Ryknield Street. Across the road is a row of modern houses and in one of these, during the 1980's, lived Michelle, her two sisters and her parents. Michelle was then in her early teens.

> One night, I was lying in bed, half asleep, when I heard what I thought was mother come into my bedroom. Someone opened the door and walked round my bed. I remember hearing the swish of coarse clothing rubbing together and I assumed it was my mother's

jeans. Then I felt two hands digging sharply into my back, just above my waist. I turned over and looked up, expecting to see my mother, but no-one was there. It gave me quite a fright.

I told my father what had happened and he said, 'Oh, the Jubilee ghost must have come across the road'. I looked at him, absolutely gob-smacked. Then we both laughed.

Michelle's mother, Diane, continues:

The Jubilee was definitely haunted during the 1980's. I don't know how Bob, the manager, lived there. I thought he was very brave. Several customers saw the ghost of a little old man sitting in the bar - that was before the bar was changed. It's more of an eating house now. In those days it had a log fire and one of the long seats that used to go round the wall, then there was a table in the corner. It was at this table that the old man was sitting. He had grey hair, so they said, and he was a bit toothless (one tooth here and there), and on the table would be a candle.

Late one winter night, after hours - I would say it was about one o'clock in the morning - there were about ten of us, friends and neighbours, sitting in the bar. All the lights were off except for those in the bar. We had been watching a big fight, the fight had finished and we had stayed on having a chat and a drink. We heard a noise and Bob said, 'What the hell is that?'. We all heard it, because we all turned round to look at the door, which had glass panels so that you could just see into the passageway beyond. We could hear whispering, and we could see the shadows of four or five girls in the passageway. Bob said, 'I bet it's somebody from the toilets' and he shot over to the door, two of the men with him. When he opened the door nobody was there. He looked round the toilets but nobody was there either. We were all flabbergasted. We said, 'What was that then?' and we were stunned, really. We thought we must be imagining things. We knew something was there but we didn't know what. We talked about it afterwards and we agreed that the girls had been wearing Victorian bonnets, the kind that are tied under the chin.

129

TARDEBIGGE

(See also *Midland Spirits and Spectres* and *Haunted Pubs in Worcestershire*)

Tardebigge church stands on a hill and the tower, built in 1777 by Francis Hiorn, overlooks the Bromsgrove Highway. A cutting from the Glastonbury thorn, said to bloom on Christmas day, is reputed to have grown in the churchyard and below the church was a spring with curative powers. At the bottom of this hill is a major feat of Victorian engineering, the country's longest flight of narrow locks, ie thirty to achieve a rise of 217 feet on a twenty-five mile stretch. A long canal tunnel starts by Tardebigge church and finishes on the other side of the B4096. As far back as anyone can remember, the tunnel has had the reputation of being haunted.

In the autumn of 1989 Margaret had a narrow boat on the canal.

There were four of us on the boat, Dave, Andrew, my husband and myself, all professional people. We had planned a day on the Tardebigge flight which has fifty-eight locks between Tardebigge and Worcester. It was the end of the day, just about dusk, we had reached the top of the flight and we moored at the Engine House.

Suddenly, we all heard someone else locking up the flight. We heard the paddle gear going which is a distinct ratchet movement, you can't mistake it. We could hear the working of the mechanics. We said to each other, 'It's a bit late to come up the locks'. (It's not considered desirable to moor anywhere between locks, in the pound). Dave and Andrew said, 'They may have children, we will go and help them'. They walked a long way down the locks and they came back gobsmacked. There was nothing, nobody there.

John Done lived on a houseboat at Tardebigge for many years.

In the evenings, the boat dwellers tend to congregate in the local pub and when the evenings are long and dark, that's when the ghost stories emerge. There are all kind of ghost stories about the tunnels, of phantom figures and of ghostly hands being pressed against the windows. You are there in the pitch dark for ages. When we go into the Tardebigge tunnel, my family all shut themselves in the cabin and switch the lights on, leaving me to steer the boat in the dark.

This story happened on Tardebigge Top Lock in the summer of 1983. Tardebigge has one of the longest flights in the country. The Top Lock is the first lock after the tunnel, it's the one you can see from the road by Lock Cottage and is unusual in that most of the other flights have a drop of six feet but the Top Lock drops down twelve feet and it takes a bit of filling up. It's about half a mile from this lock to the next one.

The incident occurred to my friend Alan when he was making his way to Stoke Works, which is at the bottom of the flight. We often take out our boats together in various rallies but on this occasion there was just his wife and himself. His wife was steering the boat . It was a big purpose-built one, about seventy feet long. The dog was locked inside. It was getting dark. He got off the boat and went round and opened the paddle at the top of the lock. It's a rack and pinion affair and to do this you have to wind the mechanism up. The rack sticks up and opens the paddle under the water. Then there's a little lever which you just push up which locks into place. Then you have to walk over the top of the lock (there is a handrail) and do the same to the other side. It takes three or four minutes to fill with water. Then you open the gate and the boat goes into the canal. The girlfriend was quite close to the lever so she also saw what happened.

The boat went into the lock which closed up again, then he wound down the paddle on the towpath side. As he dropped that one down, he went to step on the bar across with the handrail. He saw the ratchet arm on the other side come up and it locked the other side in place. The big rack that sticks up slowly went down. When you pull the catches out, it can drop quite quickly and makes a lot of noise, then the lock-keeper comes out and tells you off. You are taught to wind down slowly. He saw the ratchet come up and wind down slowly just as if someone was winding it down. He didn't feel at all afraid. He felt that someone was helping him. He was fascinated.

The huge stately home of the Earl of a Plymouth, Hewell Grange, is at Tardebigge. It is now more familiar to Her Majesty's guests as it has been converted into an open prison. Two other prisons, Blakenhurst and Brockhill, have also been built on the site.

The Worcester & Birmingham canal at Tardebigge

In 1911 The Earl of Plymouth built a village hall for the residents of Tardebigge. Built by Braziers (see The Haunted Quarry, Bromsgrove) at a cost of £5,185.0s.6d, it was called the Hewell Institute. The hall was finished just in time to be used as a military hospital during the first world war. Unfortunately, two Earls died in succession incurring heavy death duties. As the residents could not prove that the hall belonged to them, it was sold in 1946 and is now the Tardebigge Public House. (See *Haunted Pubs and Hotels*). This, also, has the reputation of being haunted.

Joy Rust worked at the Tardebigge for more than three years in the early 1990s. She says:

> All kinds of weird things happened while I was there. Things used to get turned round - you would put a knife down and when you looked at it again it would be upside down. I was standing in the bar one night when a guy came in and put his keys on the bar. About an hour later, he went to leave and he said, 'Where are my keys?'. We looked for them and eventually found them on a shelf at the back of the bar. I had been the only one working in the bar and I definitely hadn't put them there.
>
> One Sunday three other ladies and I took a load of cutlery into the function room because we had to lay up for a function of some kind. I put a handful of spoons on the table and never found them again. We just didn't know where they went. We're still looking for them.
>
> I always thought it was a nice place. It had a nice atmosphere. The ghost never used to harm anyone. I used to think it was one of the nurses from the first world war who was waiting for her boyfriend to come back.
>
> There's a little cupola on top of the Tardebigge and twice, in the late evening, just as

The Tardebigge, now a public house and restaurant with a children's play area

132

it's getting dusk, I've seen her standing there. I could only see the dark shape of a woman but I could just make out her uniform.

Iris Thomason worked behind the bar during the late 1960's when she was in her mid-thirties.

This one night I was asked for a drink which I hadn't got so I had to go down to the cellar - well, it was called the cellar but it was really a room at the back of the ballroom. Of course, it's all changed now. I went waltzing down, not a care in the world. I had to go down a little corridor which ran down the side of the old kitchen and there I saw in front of me this grey shape. It was a blue-grey mist, and the shape of a smallish woman. It was just standing there. I went on walking and I must have walked through it. I didn't think about it. I went very cold, in fact I was shivering when I went back to the bar.

Somebody at the bar said, You look as if you've seen a ghost. They said that I was grey. I said, 'Well, I think I have'. I can laugh about it now but at the time it was a little bit unnerving.

I told my dad who used to work at Hewell Grange. He said, 'Oh, that's Lady Plymouth you saw, she used to walk the wards, she was nursing there'. I have often told the children this story and they say, 'Oh granny saw a ghost'. I don't know what it was but it was certainly something very peculiar.

THE SUCKLEY HILLS

To the north-west of the Malvern hills are the gentle Suckley hills, where Alfrick once had the reputation of being the most haunted village in England. On the edge of these hills is a large, comfortable old farmhouse, with thick white-washed walls and a huge kitchen with aga and quarried floor.

The farmer , *John Davies, says:

After Pat moved in, I saw the ghost twice over a period of two years. I don't know why that should be. Perhaps it had been here all the time and Pat just made me aware of it. You only see it out of the corner of your eye, you perceive that something is there but when you look straight ahead you don't see it so clearly. Or, perhaps having a lot of people in the house livened him up. For about eight years, there was just myself and my two teenage sons, then I remarried and my wife, Pat, moved in with her four teenage daughters. It was pandemonium.

The first time I saw him he was standing in the kitchen, in front of the aga. He was a small man, well-built and elderly, well-tanned and wearing a shirt without a collar. There is an archway there and at one time it would have had a huge oven covering most of the wall. To the left and about halfway down would have been a small door, behind which was the bread oven. To use it, you lit a fire inside the oven then after it had got really hot,

133

you raked the embers out and put the bread in. He had his arms round a large bundle of peasticks and was bending slightly towards the area of the bread oven as if he was about to put them in..

A few months later I was going up the stairs and someone was coming down, I had to dodge them to get past. Then suddenly, he wasn't there. It reminded me of that poem:

The other day, upon the stair,
I met a man who wasn't there.
I wish that man would go away ...

although I didn't find him at all frightening.

Pat Davies continues:

I first saw it a few days before I married John and came to live here. I can remember that I was working in the kitchen, I looked up and there was the ghost, just in front of our aga. He was an elderly man, quite short, with a grandad-type shirt without the collar, scruffy old trousers and big farm boots. He was bending over, as if he was going to put a bundle of sticks on the aga. He was there for quite a few minutes.

The removal man also saw the ghost a few days later when we moved in. We had three men moving the furniture, an older man and two younger. It was the older man who saw the ghost. He said, 'Do you know you have a ghost? He's standing on the bend of the stairs!'. After that the two young men refused to go upstairs and they left the furniture in the yard so we had to wait until my stepsons came home to move the furniture upstairs.

A few months later we had a great housewarming party and I saw him again. Our stairs run along the side of the hall, and he was standing halfway up the stairs, watching all the people milling around down below. The last time I saw him, he was standing by the front door. The children had said, 'Do tell us when you see him!' so I went into the kitchen where three or four teenagers were hanging around and said, 'He's there now!'. There was a stampede as they all rushed to the front door, but he had gone.

We have asked the previous occupants if they ever saw anything and they didn't, although one of them said, 'Our daughter talked a lot of nonsense about playing with granpy but she did have a vivid imagination'.

We haven't seen him since 1987. In that year the man died who lived in this house before us, I often wonder if this is anything to do with it.

WARNDON

Forty years ago Warndon was a country village of a dozen houses, a derelict mansion and a run-down church. Then in 1962 the M5 arrived nearby, followed by an enormous housing development. By 1996 Warndon had about 2,500 houses and by the millennium this should rise to 4,500.

The mansion, Warndon Court, has been splendidly rebuilt and is now a private house. It dates back to 1620 but there was a house on the site before then and pottery has been found dating back to 1300. Its last resident, a farmer, lived on his own without gas or electricity and he drew his water from a well. He died in 1977 and the house remained derelict for seventeen years.

The quaint little Norman church was once approached through unfenced, ungated farm meadows and had eight members. Fortunately, one of the eight was Chris Monkhouse who was prepared to dedicate all his spare time to obtaining financial support and monitoring extensive structural repairs so that the Church could become a focus for the new community. He had joined the Church in 1975 and found it in such a state of neglect that it was necessary to sweep snow off the altar before services could begin. Now St Nicholas' Norman walls gleam with fresh white paint, the half-timbered tower is structurally sound, the box pews are carefully preserved and the thirteenth century stained glass window will last for many more centuries yet.

A building with such a long history must surely have produced a ghost or two. The locals say that an apparition drifts across the pathway in front of the church. Chris has a couple of tales to tell:

> Warndon Church once served the large farmhouse next door which was built by the famous Berkeley family. In those days, labourers were not allowed to fraternise with the gentry, and the story goes that about 1700, one of the Berkeley daughters was a bit too friendly with a farm worker. She and her lover tried to escape from the wrath of her father by running into the church, hoping that it would provide them with sanctuary, but the father caught up with them in the churchyard and shot the young farm worker. As he was the local magistrate the case never got to court. The ghost of the young lady, it is said, comes looking for her lover and in the 1960's a sighting of the ghost was reported by the *Worcester Evening News* two or three times.
>
> A second ghost story goes back to 1926, when some essential repairs were being made to the structure of the fabric. A plasterer was working halfway up a ladder, with his mate mixing the plaster outside, when a figure in a black cloak and a cardinal's hat with a big flat rim walked from the vestry to the altar, did something at the altar and glided back to the vestry. When the terrified plasterer managed to unglue himself from the ladder he asked his mate if he had seen anyone entering the vestry. The mate replied that he

hadn't seen anyone but the plasterer was very sceptical and from that day to this we don't know whether it was one of his workmates playing a joke or the real thing.

Warndon church is in the foreground with Warndon Court behind.

WORCESTERSHIRE - GENERAL

The narrators of the last four stories have all asked for their names not to be revealed and because the houses or events in the story are so unusual, we have been unable to give a precise area.

The everlasting cross

About twenty years ago we bought an old vicarage from the Worcestershire Church Commissioners. When we moved in, we found that over the fireplace in the lounge, was the outline of a cross, about nine inches deep by about six inches across. When we decorated, we painted over it but to our surprise it showed through. We hung a gilt mirror over it and forgot about it.

A few years later we sold the house to an architect. We said to him, 'We're sorry about the mark of the cross over the fireplace' and we told him that we had tried to cover it up. He told us not to worry, he would strip the plaster down to the bricks and get rid of it that way.

A couple of years ago he sold the house to some mutual friends and we went to visit them. There, over the fireplace, was the outline of a cross. We remarked on this and they told us that the architect had tried everything to get rid of it, he had stripped the plaster and used every kind of covering but each time the silhouette of the cross had returned. Wasn't that strange?

A rich man's castle

This is a wealthy businessman's house. Part stone, part half-timbered, no-one knows when it was first built, only that it was a farmhouse and that the size of it indicates a landowner of some importance. The present owner, Stuart*, has restored it with imagination and flair and to add to its character it also has a manifestation of some kind.

Stuart, who lives with his young son, tells his story after supper. The huge dining room is reminiscent of a medieval banqueting hall, with an oak table almost as long as the room, oak rafters, stone walls and a slate slab floor covered by animal skins.

I bought this house when it needed a lot of repair and the last two years have been spent restoring it. Then about fourteen months ago, I was having a very vivid dream when I suddenly woke up to find myself being pulled out of bed. I started screaming. My son, who was then aged about eight, happened to be sleeping with me; he sat bolt upright and asked what the matter was. I told him to go back to sleep. A bit later that night, probably about twenty minutes later, I heard my ex-wife's voice calling me very plainly twice. She seemed to be standing at the bottom of the stairs.

A few weeks ago I was woken up by murmuring which seemed to be above me or behind me and I felt as if someone was sitting on the bed. I switched on the light and I saw depressions being made on the bed, as if an invisible somebody was sitting there. Then I heard a scraping noise, as if somebody was dragging a load of concrete over the floor-boards. This was going on in another room, I don't know where.

Another night I was in bed and I distinctly heard someone come in through the front door. It is fitted with draft excluders which make a distinct swishing noise. I heard the front door open and footsteps approach. At first they were muffled as they walked on the carpet, then they rang out when they reached the stone floor. The door closed again. I thought I must have left the front door open and someone had come in but when I had a look at it in the morning it was locked.

I'm not the only one who experiences things. One Saturday morning three friends were in one of the rooms, two of them were playing chess. They were talking and laughing then suddenly, everything went quiet. I looked in to make sure everything was alright and I saw three white faces staring at me. The door had slowly opened and closed all by itself.

An incident occurs about once a fortnight. Most of them are quite trivial, the lights flicker, or they don't work at all for no reason. Things go missing - I'm a very neat and tidy person and, for example, I know that I put the complete corkscrew opener in the kitchen drawer but half of it has disappeared. Also, I found a pile of obituary cards in the attic and the one referring to a previous resident of the house has removed itself from the pile and still hasn't turned up. I have an old-fashioned bedpan which I use for the ashes and someone banged on it just as if it was a drum. I was standing in the hall one Saturday morning with the carpenter when one of the balls of the chandelier moved quickly backwards and forwards, as if someone had given it a good push. One night I was out on the patio and I head three footsteps loudly and clearly behind me. I turned round but no-one was there.

I could put up with all these things but a few days ago I was woken up by someone pinching my arm. Enough is enough. I have put the house up for sale.

Unknown modes of being

Betty* is a widow with two sons. The older one, John, is in his mid-twenties and a lorry driver but the younger one, Daniel, died tragically in a road accident when in his late teens.

Since that time, we have had so many strange things happening, that I don't know where to begin.

I turn the lights off at night and they're on in the morning, I turn the TV off and that's also on. The video suddenly starts rewinding for no reason. Sometimes the dog sees something I don't, his ears go up. Early one morning I was on the telephone to a friend, sitting there in my nightdress and looking for an excuse to bring the conversation to a close when all of a sudden the light went off. I stood up to turn the light back on and it came on of its own accord. It didn't flicker, it was a definite on and off.

A week or two ago, I had only been in the house five minutes when the telephone rang. A man said, 'I have just come home and I have dialled 1471 and your number has come up'. I told him that it couldn't have been me, I had been out all day. Later that day a friend of mine, who is disabled, phoned me and said, 'What did you want?'. He said that the telephone had rung while he was in the loo, so when he was able he had dialled 1471 and again, my number had come up.

When a friend of mine, a mature lady, was here, the lounge door kept creaking open. She said, 'I don't like that'. I was in the kitchen when the phone went and, as the phone is in the hall, she called out, 'I'll get that'. She went to push the door open and she couldn't. She said, 'There's someone pushing from the other side'. We couldn't open it, we had to leave the telephone to ring. A little later the door opened without any diffi-culty. The atmosphere in here that day was awful. I didn't like it at all. Usually, the atmos-phere is nice, I'm in the house on my own and I'm not frightened.

I have heard my teenage son run up the stairs twice. Then last week or the week before, I was washing up in the kitchen and John was outside messing about with the car, when I turned round and saw someone who I thought was John walk through the door. A few minutes later I went out the front of the house and I said to him, 'Crikey, you have changed quickly'. He told me that he had been wearing those clothes all morning. I said, 'I have just seen you come through that door with all your black clothes on'. Daniel always wore black.

After the accident I was packed off on holiday. John was alone in the house and asleep upstairs when he was woken up by what he thought was a burglary. It sounded as if someone was throwing furniture about. He came downstairs and the noise stopped, then he got to the top of the stairs and it started again. So he went into the bedroom, closed the door and went back to sleep again.

John had two overnight deliveries to make which meant staying out at all night. When he went out he locked the back door and hung the keys up. When he came back the following morning the door was unlocked and the keys were still hanging up. The next night he took the keys with him. The following morning the door was wide open.

He had to drive to a depot near Bristol where a worker helped him to load and unload. He got into the cab and was driving off when the worker said, 'Don't go without your young lad!'. John said, 'I haven't got a young lad' to which the man replied, 'You have, he has just got out of the cab and walked down the side of the lorry'. The man noticed John's surprise, and added that the young lad was dressed in black with black hair which was long at the front, over his eyes, and short at the back. That was Daniel down to a T.

On another journey he had to go to a depot where he had to reverse in on the blind side. There was this young lad beckoning him in. John thought, 'He looks just like Daniel'. When the lorry was safely in position he went off to make a cup of tea for himself and the lad but the young man had disappeared. He thought nothing of it and sat in his cab doing his bookwork but he happened to look in the mirror and there was the young lad again. The young lad walked up to the lorry and disappeared through the side.

All John's friends have experienced something or other. One of his friends, Alan, had a hat that lifted itself off the top of his wardrobe and floated down on to the bed. He assumed that Daniel was making his presence felt. Susan, Daniel's girlfriend, has felt him stroking her hair. Another friend, Ben, came to keep me company but I had to pop out. Ben had only been left alone here for ten minutes when he saw Daniel get out of a chair and come towards him with his hand raised and his index finger extended. Daniel walked straight through Ben and as he went he patted Ben's shoulder. Ben said that he wasn't frightened, he took it that Daniel was saying, 'thank you' for looking after me.

Another time I was about three miles from home with John and our car conked out. I phoned his ex-girl-friend for the number of our local mechanic. She was out so her mother brought along her brother who knew quite a bit about cars. He discovered that the car had a faulty petrol gauge so that a can of petrol did the trick. When he got home he was just going off to sleep when the music centre suddenly turned itself on and started playing loud music. He was scared but he took it that it was Daniel saying, 'Thank you'.

When I tell people about these strange happenings they say, 'Aren't you scared?'. But I'm not, in fact they are a great comfort to me. I am now absolutely positive that there is an after-life.

Whispers and giggles

These next incidents occurred in a house which is thought to be at least four hundred years old and which has now been converted into bed-sitters for students. David, one of the students, explains:

It began not long after we moved in, late in 1987. Doors started opening by themselves - the bathroom door would open as you went down the stairs towards it. Things that I was putting down in my room were being moved. I would put a comb on a chest of drawers and the next minute it would be on the bed. Whenever I went to bed I would feel that someone was watching me. As soon as I started going off to sleep I would sense that something was there.

Then one night, I was asleep on my side, facing the wall, when I felt a poke in my back. I had been asleep for some time so that it must have been in the early hours. It was a strong poke, halfway down my back, enough to wake me up. I was very shocked. The next night I was poked again, and these pokes and pinches not only continued but increased until I was getting very little rest. I didn't see anything, I just felt these pinches. After a few weeks of this, I had to move my bed on to the landing so that I could get some sleep.

Another student, Alice slept in my room one night to see if anything happened to her. Although she was left alone, she woke up in the night to see the shadows of a group of people standing by the chest of drawers.

The disturbances were such a nuisance that the two students involved, *David and *Alice, asked the Society for Psychical Research for help. Margaret Webb went to see them and said later that although she couldn't see anything, she could hear a great deal, it sounded like a party. At least eight young girls were in the room and there was much swishing of skirts and female giggling. They evidently wanted to play with this handsome young man and refused to let him go to sleep. Margaret said that she spoke to them and told them that they should go back to their own world where there were many more handsome young men.

Margaret's strategy seemed to have worked because the young man has been able to move back into his room. The two students were intrigued by this experience and have been investigating the history of the house. They discovered that during the latter half of the last century, the house was used as a girl's reformatory.

BIBLIOGRAPHY

In addition to local guides and reference books, the following have been especially useful:

The Victoria County History, A History of the County of Worcestershire, published for the University of London Institute of Historical Research, 1913.

The Worcestershire Village Book, reprinted 1992, published jointly by Countryside Books, Newbury, and the WFWI, Worcester.

Avery William. *The William Avery Memorial Volumes*, Volume !, collated cuttings from Redditch Indicator and other local newspapers 1823-1899 (in Redditch library).

Bradford Anne *Haunted Worcestershire*,1996 and *Haunted Pubs and Hotels of Worcestershire and its Borders*, 1998, both by Hunt End Books.

Bradford Anne and Roberts Barrie, *Midland Ghosts and Hauntings* (1997) and *Midland Spirits and Spectres* (1998) by Quercus.

Greenwood Mary and Morford Frances, *A Children's History of Worcestershire*, 1955, Ebenezer Baylis & Son Ltd.

Palmer Roy, *The Folklore of Hereford and Worcester*, 1992, Logaston Press.

Pevsner Niklaus, *Worcestershire*, from the Buildings of England series, reprinted 1985, Penguin.

Other books used have been listed in the text.